The FREEDOM SEEKER

RUCHIRA GUPTA

SCHOLASTIC PRESS

Library of Congress Cataloging-in-Publication Data available

ISBN 978-93-5954-254-6

This reprint edition May 2026
Book design by Maithili Joshi
Printed in India at Shivam Offset Press, New Delhi

For all those seeking home
in a tumultuous world—may you find safety,
dignity, and the freedom to belong.

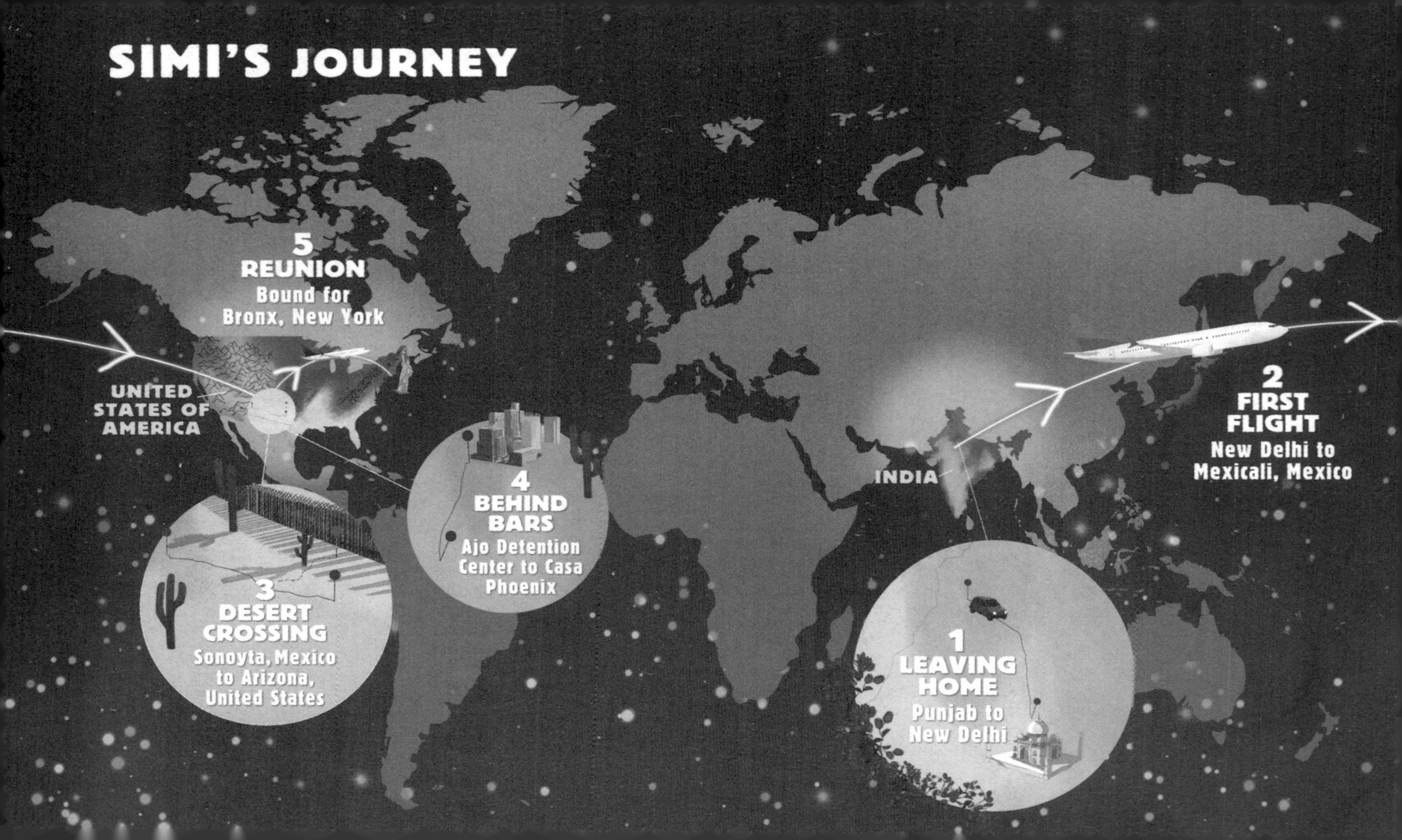
SIMI'S JOURNEY
1
LEAVING HOME
Punjab to New Delhi
INDIA
2
FIRST FLIGHT
New Delhi to Mexicali, Mexico
3
DESERT CROSSING
Sonoyta, Mexico to Arizona, United States
4
BEHIND BARS
Ajo Detention Center to Casa Phoenix
5
REUNION
Bound for Bronx, New York
UNITED STATES OF AMERICA

1

Fear and Flight

CHAPTER ONE

Ammi sings with her head tilted back, her braid flying in the air. The blue ribbon at its end flutters like butterfly wings. The morning sun turns the handles of her bicycle to gold.

We ride our bikes over the grass, making mad patterns, looping around, then racing to see who reaches the end of the lane first. We swerve off the tarmac toward a patch of green sparkling with dewdrops.

"Doe . . . a deer . . ."

She's been singing this song to me for as long as I can remember.

I'm on my way to school and Ammi to the hospital, where she's head nurse in the outpatient department. There are no cars on the street this early in the morning. A sidewalk divides the grass from the road. The orange-red flowers on the gulmohar trees look as happy as we do.

Ammi pauses with a smile. Her nurse's uniform sparkles a silvery white. Our bicycle wheels whir cheerfully while we trade lyrics back and forth. If people saw us from a distance, they would think we were two sisters instead of mother and daughter.

I'm almost as tall as Ammi. We're both slender with long black hair. I've tied mine in a single braid just like hers but with a red ribbon at the end to match the red skirt of my school uniform.

We cycle quietly for the next few minutes to let the breeze cool our flushed faces. An orange petal flutters up the rough pathway that leads to the school gate as we reach the fork where we must part. I drag my right toe along the gray tarred road to slow down and almost bump into a roly-poly ball.

"Yawp!!!"

I jump back as the ball squeaks, and I realize that it's a teeny-tiny puppy. Instinctively, I pick up the soft bundle of brown fur and cuddle it.

"He's such a baby. Look at his eyes. We can keep him, can't we, Ammi?" I ask, clutching it close to my chest. Ammi begins to nod a "yes."

But a loud growl interrupts our plan. A skinny brown dog has come out of nowhere. It stares at us, hair on end, teeth bared.

"I think we have to return the puppy to its mother," Ammi says.

I hold the small creature a bit tighter. "Ammi, please! I can look after it better. I'll be able to give it more food than its mother. Please let me keep her," I cry.

"But the mother needs her baby, Simi. Don't you think?" Ammi asks, nodding her head toward the dog, who steps closer.

I bend down slowly and put the puppy back on the ground even though it's the last thing I want to do. The mother rushes over and washes her puppy thoroughly before snuggling it to her belly.

"When will . . . I mean . . . I really . . . why can't—" I stumble through a jumble of questions as I mount the bike again.

"That's quite a number of unfinished sentences!" Ammi laughs as she covers my left hand on the handlebar with her palm. "Explain slowly."

"I just wish I could keep it," I say with a deep sigh.

"Would you be happy to be away from *me*?" asks Ammi, her head to one side.

I consider this for a moment, turning over in my mind the idea of life without Ammi.

"No. No, not even for a day," I answer, heaving another sigh.

"It's the same for us. Abbu and I can't live a day without you."

Abbu, my father, is a farmer like Dadu—his father. And a champion field hockey player too. He had tripped over a hockey stick at a match the day he met Ammi. Ammi was the nurse who bandaged him. Theirs is a love marriage.

They've told me the story a hundred times when we're

alone, when they come to tuck me in bed. "It was your father's gentle laugh and carefree air that attracted me more than anything else," Ammi always says with a smile, sitting on a corner of the bed.

Abbu always says that he knew she would be his wife the moment he looked into her large gray eyes. "I felt no sting while she put the antiseptic on my wounds. Her eyes were like our pond on the farm, still and calm."

Abbu's name is Gurbeer Singh. Ammi's is Henna Ali. They named me Simran, which is both an Arabic and Sanskrit word. It means "one who meditates." Everyone calls me Simi.

I definitely don't take after my name. I never sit still, let alone meditate. My skin has turned from pink to brown, thanks to all the field hockey practice with Abbu. I'm happiest on the hockey field. I'm nothing like Ammi, who is perfectly content to sit with a book, a crossword, or a piece of embroidery.

Her gray eyes look at me now, full of love and concern, guessing what's passing through my mind.

"How about you make friends with it, instead of

adopting it?" Ammi says. "You can give it food and water every day on your way to school?"

I grin so wide my cheeks hurt. Ammi helps me fill a little plastic cup with water from my bottle, and we give mother and baby an egg sandwich from her tiffin.

They devour the gift. The mother thumps the ground ecstatically with her big tail while the pup shakes a small stub.

Ammi always takes care of things in the best possible way. I watch as she checks the time and sees how close it is to the start of the school day.

She pulls me into a tight hug and I get back on my bike.

"See you tonight, Ammi," I say with a wave as I turn toward school.

Ammi blows flying kisses to me as she leaves for the hospital. The bike wobbles beneath me as I try to catch them.

The crowd outside of school is loud as children arrive for class—everyone waving, talking, calling at the same time.

"Simiiiiiii!" I hear Ravi's voice at full pitch above the usual morning sounds of running feet, banging doors, and loud shrieks of laughter. "Come on, hurry up," he yells again.

Ravi, my best friend, dances impatiently by the wrought iron gates. I realize just how late I am when I see he's already put his book away and returned to the real world. With his spiky hair, round steel frames, and a nose that takes up most of his face, there are times when he looks more like a hedgehog than a boy.

"Finally! I thought you might have been out sick!" Ravi says as the bell rings. We tear along the path, up the school steps to the classroom. There is the scraping of chairs and desks as students settle in. Some are chatting in groups of two or three. A girl is frantically finishing her homework, and I thank Ammi for making me do all of mine on time as usual.

"I'm done for. I haven't written the essay or done any of the math homework we were supposed to do this weekend," Ravi says as we go to our seats in the first row. He's always late with his homework, his nose mostly buried in a different book each week.

Reena, my other best friend, smirks as we slide in next to her. Her pigtails swing on both sides of her plump face. She is neat and punctual. A rule follower. Ravi and I can never fathom what she sees in us. But somehow the three of us are inseparable.

I grin at her as I shake my head in aggravation and pull out my math homework. I'm good at math and English, unlike Abbu who is hopeless at accounts. He says numbers and books are not for him. I help both Dadu and Abbu tally their farm produce and market sales.

"Here you go," I say under my breath to Ravi, sliding my homework toward him. "At least you can avoid an incomplete from Mrs. Raina."

"If I can copy the answers without anyone looking," he whispers back with a grin.

I remember when our first-grade teacher made this strange creature come and sit next to me. I didn't want to make friends with Ravi at all. Instead, I slid my pencil box between us. He didn't seem to notice though. He was always engrossed in some book. That Friday, the teacher had asked us to bring our favorite book for a reading hour, and Ravi brought a children's collection of Sherlock Holmes stories. I so wanted to read them, but there was no way I could ask after ignoring him all week.

When I reached home, I found the first book of the collection in my school bag. That was four years ago. Since then, we do everything together.

Ravi's pencil scrapes against his notebook as Miss Sharma, our class teacher, marks attendance. She calls for silence. "I have some news today," she says, her eyes locking onto mine.

I squirm in my seat, fearing she's caught me handing my math homework to Ravi. As I mentally scramble for excuses, Miss Sharma's piercing gaze holds the room in tense anticipation.

"You, Simi, have been selected by our coach to be the captain of the middle school hockey team," she announces, a rare smile spreading across her face.

My shoulders sag with relief, and my cheeks warm as I part my lips in a surprised smile. I start to stand to express my thanks, but she raises a hand to stop me. "And there's more," she continues. "Your team will participate in the inter-school hockey competition in Delhi this year."

She pauses to ensure she has everyone's attention. "I am making this announcement not just to celebrate Simi's achievement but also because it will affect everyone here. The team's preparation and travel will impact our class schedule and some joint activities with other classes."

Thud-thud-thud, duth, duth, duth . . . My heartbeat flip-flops with excitement. Delhi! A competition in the capital city! This is indeed an honor, beyond my imagination. Some of the other kids cheer.

Miss Sharma continues with announcements, detailing the term's quiz competitions, the names of other students selected for the hockey team, the end-of-term dance, and the cultural program. Her role as class teacher includes coordinating these activities and making sure that everything is balanced with our academic schedule.

Ravi and Reena whisper their congratulations. They know more than anyone how badly I've wanted this. I come to my senses, stand up, and thank Miss Sharma. She tells me I'm scheduled to meet the headmistress during recess.

As Miss Sharma hands out the pop quiz sheets, I'm miles away, sprinting across the hockey field in my mind. I smack the ball into the net, and the sound of "Hurrah! Hurrah!" fills my ears, making me grin.

Whoosh!

A paper airplane crashes onto my desk, pulling me back to the classroom. I glance around. Everyone's heads are down, pencils scratching feverishly on paper. They didn't see it. I pick up the paper plane and tease it open. The message inside punches me in the gut:

Go back where you belong, Paki.

Heat crawls up my face. I squeeze the paper hard, crumpling it in my fist. My eyes scan the room. Ashok is smirking at me, his pimply face twisted in a nasty sneer.

My heart kicks against my chest like it wants to escape.

Should I throw it back? Tell Miss Sharma? I want to do something—maybe I could just stick my tongue out at him.

But then I remember I'm the team captain now, which is something I've always wanted to be. I've got to act like it.

I take a deep breath, chuck his mean note in the trash, and turn away from him to show him I don't care about his words. Then I just stare at the blackboard and start writing again, pretending I'm focused on the quiz. I won't let him ruin my day.

But as the period passes, my joy turns to fear. How could I possibly be a good captain? What if the team doesn't listen to me?

I wanted to make my family proud of me, to show the other kids that I was like any of them, even better. But I'd forgotten about Ashok. About all the other boys just like him. I almost wish I could give this honor back. Maybe I can. I have a pleasant enough life without it—birthdays, Diwali and Eid festivals, harvest celebrations, school exams, and hockey competitions. Maybe that's enough.

In math class, Mrs. Raina can clearly tell that I'm distracted, because she continues to call on me for answers. I reply vaguely to one algebra question after the next.

"If you can't do better than this, you had better come to me after class," Mrs. Raina declares. "I'll be happy to give you some extra homework to clear these concepts."

I take a deep breath and order myself to go through the rest of the lesson without letting Ashok's note mess with my head. Luckily, Ravi saves me by making a complete hash of his formula so that Mrs. Raina's attention is diverted to him. I look down at my book fiercely and decide, once again, that I will not let Ashok's heckling get to me.

When class is over at last, somebody shakes my hand to congratulate me. One girl asks me to autograph her book. I feel the anger begin to recede as I sign my name with a flourish.

Ravi and Reena are already waiting impatiently at the door of the classroom. We share a quick lunch from each other's boxes in the corner of the yard behind the shed.

"Revenge!" Reena declares when I tell her about Ashok's note.

We list all the different ways we can get back at him.

Ravi says he can put some varnish on the seat of Ashok's chair. "He won't even know, and then his shorts will be stained!"

We chortle at the idea.

I lift my head. "No. I'm a captain now. I have to lead by example. 'Courage, confidence, and excellence,'" I say, repeating the school motto. "I won't do anything underhanded."

CHAPTER TWO

Tonight at our family's Eid festival celebration, I have more reason than ever to celebrate.

Dadi, my father's mother, opens the lid of her heirloom gramophone and places the needle on a vinyl record.

"Ina mina dika . . . Daye dama neeka . . . Maka naka naka." A melody from an old Bollywood movie fills our living room. Dadu, my father's father, taps his walking stick to the music. The evening sun filters through the open French windows, casting a pinkish light on the Persian carpet inside. The silver dots on

Ammi's new blue salwar kameez catch the sparkle of the rays as she loads sweets onto the side table.

My grandparents on my mother's side—Nani, my beloved grandmother, and Nanaji, my ever-hungry grandfather—arrive with kebabs made of lamb chunks marinated in spiced yogurt.

Everyone settles into the deep armchairs upholstered with floral chintz cloth. Ammi and I had recently found the pretty fabric in the new mall.

Nanaji tucks into a kebab. Abbu teases him, warning him of weight gain. Nanaji argues with great authority, "I don't put on weight from kebabs. It's only butter chicken that makes me round."

"That's not scientific," my mother challenges her doctor father with a laugh. Nanaji's black eyes twinkle behind his thick black glasses as he leans forward to dip yet another kebab into the green mint chutney.

I look at everyone—eating, chatting, joking, laughing together. It's the perfect moment for the big news. I take a deep breath to still my heart. Then I clap my hands to get everyone's attention.

"Are you going to sing a song, Simi, beta? Should I shut the gramophone?" Dadi asks.

I shake my head, drawing in my breath, conscious of my heart swelling with pride. I trot out the words in a rush.

"I have news." All eyes are on me. "Meet the captain of the middle school hockey team," I say, bowing with a flourish.

The whole room is a smile. Nani's eyes are bright, her cheeks red with excitement. She holds out a hand to me. "Come here, Simi. Let me give you a kiss! I am so proud of you."

Abbu pats me on the back. His eyes glint with pride as he says, "Now I have a chance to score a goal against the captain."

I flex my muscles and say, "No chance. My team will fend you off."

Ammi slips an arm around my waist, her gray eyes gleaming with happiness as she leans close to my ear. "I'm so happy for you," she says.

Dadu, tall and strapping like Abbu, with the same love

for colorful turbans and over-the-top laughter, cheers.

Suddenly, I'm too embarrassed to speak. Then I disgrace myself by burying my head in Ammi's shoulder and bursting into tears. Suddenly, I'm crying like I haven't in ages. All the emotions that brewed throughout the day today suddenly flood out.

What if I'm not good at it? What if my teammates rebel, gang up against me?

"You will be a fantastic captain," Ammi says, holding me close. It's as though she can read my thoughts.

"By the time you were six, you were already a leader in school and at home," Dadu reminds me. "Remember how you invented word games for your friends. With unheard-of expressions? It set everyone into fits of laughter. They all wanted to be around you."

"I don't have enough time." I hiccup as my sobs slow down. "There's dance practice for the cultural program, and end-of-term exams, and . . ."

"Is it too much for you?" Ammi asks. "Are you too tired? Would you like to give something up?"

I do love dance practice. And nothing can replace the

deep satisfaction of solving a math problem in class before anyone else.

"Not really. It's just . . ."

I don't tell them what I'm actually thinking about—about Ashok. That he called me a Pakistani. I know I'm as Indian as him. I was born in this city, in this country like my mother and father and their mothers and fathers and their mothers and fathers before them.

Ammi squeezes my shoulder. "I will meet your teachers and see how we can lighten your schedule."

I wipe my tears as Abbu thumps me on the back. "Come, come, champs. Don't cry."

Looking up at Abbu, I think about the Delhi championship—it's the All-India National Youth Gold Cup. Winning there means getting to play in bigger, international games, and it's also where the big-time coaches look for new stars for national teams.

Abbu used to be a national champ, before he got hurt. Winning could kind of be like finishing what he started, and it's my dream too. I can do it, I know I can, especially if I lead the team right.

I brush away the last tear and straighten up tall, ready to show Ashok and any other bully that I'm not backing down. I'm here to play hockey, win big, and make Abbu proud. No one's mean words can stop me.

I imagine running across the field, hockey stick in hand, the crowd cheering as I swoop past defenders and slap the ball into the net. No bully, no taunt can hold me back. Not when I've got this much excitement bubbling through me. I'm all set to kick off this adventure.

I grin at my family.

Dadi holds out her arms. "Come. Let's dance. I'll teach you the twist. It was very popular when I was in college."

She throws her left hand up in the air, snapping her fingers to the rhythm, holding her balance with a walking stick in the other hand.

I follow her moves. I twist to the left then to the right, tripping up and down the silk Persian carpet. I'm about to twist way down, almost to the floor, when something crashes through the window into our living room.

I jump back with a shriek, straight into the small table with the jug of lemonade.

"Coo-ooooo," a koel bird cries.

A car horn screeches. As the car drives away, I see the bumper sticker reads COMBAM in large orange letters. My heart closes in and my toes curl inside my new silver slippers.

The lemonade has spread across the tiny pink flowers on my new kameez, a twelfth birthday gift from Ammi. My mother had carefully embroidered each flower. I watched her draw the thread through the cloth, in and out, in and out, as she told me stories about her childhood. My job was to snip and needle the thread and help match the colors from the embroidery skeins. Each flower is connected to a family story.

It seems everyone in the room has stopped breathing. Dadi lifts the needle off the vinyl record and shuts the lid on the gramophone. The smile on her face is gone. Her tiny plump body is rigid as she turns toward Ammi.

Ammi's eyes darken as she slowly leans down to pick up the rock, wrapped up in a piece of white paper. A wrinkle appears just below the matching blue bindi on her forehead as she straightens.

Abbu's bushy eyebrows have come together. He takes the rock from Ammi's hand and slowly unties the string around it, unfolds the paper, and reads aloud. *"Cancel marriage between Sikh man and Muslim woman. Sikh and Hindu men are being lured to Islam with marriage. We will punish you. Go home, beef eaters."*

My father's face puckers into a scowl. The silence is deathly. I want someone to say something, anything. The hush is broken by Ammi's sobs. Nani keeps twisting the end of her silk sari into knots.

My palms hurt from my nails digging in.

I run to Ammi and put my arms around her. She holds me close. Eventually, I notice that Dadu and Dadi, Nanaji and Nani have all pulled their chairs closer to Ammi. Nani is holding Ammi's free hand in a tight clasp as Abbu hovers over us.

Dadu pats Ammi's back. "We are among intolerant people. Times are changing. But it will pass," he says, letting out a long sigh.

"Will it?" asks Nanaji softly, polishing the lenses of his spectacles.

"Yes, of course it will," Dadi insists, her back upright, assertive.

"I just don't get it," I say. "You're happy. *We're* happy. What makes your marriage wrong to these people?" I ask, bewildered, staring at the faces of my family. I pull my braid to the front and play with the ribbon as I wait for some grown-up to explain why it matters to these people that Ammi is Muslim.

Nobody answers for a moment.

"Even we don't understand," Ammi says with a sad shake of her head, her wobbly voice becoming stronger as she adds, "Love between people is never wrong. Only hate is wrong."

The rock is lying on the coffee table next to the pile of colorfully wrapped gifts for the Eid festival, its evil eye turned toward all of us.

Across the room, our beautifully sculpted terra-cotta Ganesh statue stares back at me. Nanaji had gifted it to Ammi when he came back from a work trip to Odisha. I shut my eyes and pray silently to the elephant god. *Please remove all obstacles from our path.*

He says nothing.

Ammi comes to my room. I pretend to be reading a book. Her hand reaches out for mine as she sits at the edge of my bed.

"Simi, don't worry. We're a family. No one can tell us that our being a family is wrong."

I smile as Ammi's gentle face brings back a sense of warmth. The room begins to feel safe and cozy. But there's still so much that I don't understand.

"What's COMBAM?" I want her to tell me the truth.

She sighs, takes the book out of my hand, and puts it on the side table.

"Do you remember that incident you had with the group of boys in the park down the road?"

I sigh. I want to forget. It's been almost a year, but the memory still makes me jumpy. I give a careless shrug so

Ammi won't know how scared I really am of those stupid boys.

I had stopped when I saw them, a group of boys in brown shorts saluting an orange flag. They were getting ready to form a circle for a game of kho-kho and I had asked if I could join. A big brownish-haired boy a head taller than me had stepped forward. "Girls aren't allowed," he had said, putting his palms out in a firm "no" gesture.

If they had said yes, I could have shown them that girls were equally good at kho-kho. I had been about to open my mouth to say so when another boy started to holler:

Mozzy, Mozzy,
Mozzy daughter,
Go to your country,
Across the border.

Soon the other boys had taken up the chant. In an instant, I was encircled. I had covered my ears and looked for an escape route through the group of jeering boys.

Before I realized what I was doing, I had flung my right leg into one boy's shins. The boy had collapsed just long enough for me to escape through a gap in the suffocating circle.

I remember running all the way home.

Later, Ammi would tell me that Mozzy is a slang word for "Muslim." "And not in a good way," she had added, in a tone that told me it was the end of the conversation.

Until today.

I clasp Ammi's hand as I wait for her to go on. "They are part of a group that is against interfaith marriages. Marriages between people who practice different religions. It's called COMBAM. They want our country cleansed," she explains.

A tear drops from her eye onto my cheek as she adds, "COMBAM stands for Committee to Ban Marriages to Muslims."

I am gripped by a sense of panic. "Why is it called cleansing?"

The sweet smell of the frangipani tree outside drifts through my window. A cloud swallows the moon, and the room becomes darker.

"This group wants Muslims to leave India. That

is what they mean by cleansing," Ammi says.

I realize then that it's Ammi that they want to cleanse.

"But I'm Sikh and Hindu and Muslim. You were born here in Punjab, just like Abbu, Dadu, Dadi, Nanaji, and Nani. We are all Punjabis," I argue back.

Ammi does not answer. She holds my hands for a long time until she thinks I have fallen asleep. As soon as she tiptoes out of the room, I open my eyes again and wait until I can hear her bedroom door shut. I wait until I'm sure she is safe.

I don't know why my heart is beating faster than usual, but somehow I know that my life is about to change.

CHAPTER THREE

I wake early. For a second, I don't know why. I don't even have an exam today.

I sit at the edge of my bed, taking in the view from my window. Everything is prettier now than it is later in the day when the sun is fully up. The sky is tinged pink, and a faint bluish-white haze hangs over everything.

And then, as the smell of Abbu's morning coffee wafts into the room, I remember the rock. The fear returns. Coach says that the best captains not only lead by example but also learn to be patient and take the time to understand their opponent. But how do you even begin to understand people capable of something so cruel?

I dress quickly in blue jeans and my favorite faded cotton T-shirt, tie my hair in a quick ponytail, and rush to Abbu, banging the door hard behind me.

"Good morning," he says with a smile. "You are never going to learn to close a door gently."

Ammi walks into the kitchen in a freshly washed salwar kameez, her waist-length hair already combed and braided. But I can't help noticing the dark circles under her puffy eyes.

Abbu hands me a plate with a poached egg. The kettle boils and steam bubbles from the spout.

I put a few tea leaves into two porcelain china cups, pour the water, add milk and sugar but do not stir, just the way Ammi likes it. I look at the leaves at the bottom of the cup to foresee my future. The brown leaves turn darker and blotchier.

Abbu goes off to get ready for the farm. The earlier he gets there, the more work he can get done before it gets too hot. I can hear the tinkling of Dadi's small prayer bell as I look out of the kitchen window. She is watering the tulsi plant. She lights a small Diya and places it on the redbrick structure that encloses the plant. She then snaps her fingers three times before plucking a few leaves. She says the sound will prepare the plant for the pain.

Soon, Dadi will give us each a spoonful of water infused with the tulsi leaves. Dadi believes the tulsi is a manifestation of Laxmi, the Hindu goddess of prosperity. This simple ritual reassures me. We are Hindu and Sikh and Muslim. Surely all these gods will protect Ammi and my family.

A sob rises in my throat, because for now, everything precious is normal again.

Math is still math. Literature is still literature. Classes continue as usual. But the school's hallways feel different. They seem to echo with the whispers of students. I imagine I overhear snippets about me, about the "girl captain" from an interfaith background.

There's no way she's going to keep the boys in line.

They'll walk all over her by the end of the week.

Just wait till the first match. She'll crumble and they'll have to rethink this whole "girl power" stunt.

I keep walking, my books clutched like a shield.

At lunch, I sit with Ravi and Reena. "Did you guys see the note they put on my locker?" I ask, trying to keep my voice even. I can still picture it on the inside of my eyelids with every blink.

Go home, Captain Simi

Ravi looks furious, but Reena squeezes my hand. "Ignore them, Simi. They're just trying to get to you. We know you're more than capable."

I nod, feeling the weight of their expectations. "I have to be," I admit. For the team. For myself. "Coach says a team leader has to be positive, thoughtful, and show no fear."

I don't tell them about the rock, or how long it took for me to fall asleep last night after Ammi left, as if staying awake would somehow protect her. I don't tell them how scared I am for tomorrow, my first practice as captain.

I grip my hockey stick tighter, cloaked by the chill in the air. It's early in the morning and the field is misty and silent except for the cawing of crows. The grass, slick with dew, brushes against my shoes. I inhale the fresh scent.

As captain, it's my duty to mold this group into a unified team—no easy task with just a few months looming until the Delhi tournament and every eye on me, questioning my leadership.

Ashok and his cronies lean against the goalposts, their mockery slicing through the quiet. "Think you're up for this, Simi? Or do we need to bring in your father to lead?" Ashok calls out with a sneer.

I feel the sting, but I stand my ground.

"Let's start with some drills," I tell my team, ignoring

him. "I want sharp, quick exchanges—keep the ball moving and communicate clearly. Let's build some rhythm," I announce, clapping my hands to set the pace.

The players line up, and I kick off the drill, sending the ball skimming across the dew-slick grass to Ravi, who redirects it to Reena. The ball moves crisply from player to player, the sound of sticks striking a steady beat drowns out any lingering gossip about me. I move among them, correcting stances, praising effort and techniques.

"Keep your passes low and quick, and always be ready to receive," I instruct. "Think of each pass as part of a conversation—you need to be clear and direct to be understood."

But as much as I try, whenever I attempt to give Ashok and his friends direction or even praise, they look away as if they can't hear me.

"Good effort, Karan! Next time, aim for the outer post," I yell as a shot flies wide of the goal. When another player hesitates too long with the ball, I advise, "Quick decisions, Maya! If you're under pressure, pass it off!"

I pull the team into a huddle during a water break. "You're all doing great. But hockey is about teamwork." I look around at everyone. My eyes linger on Ashok. "We need to trust each other. And once we have the trust, we need to hang on to it. Let's keep talking out there."

The team nods, their faces flushed from practice. But Ashok refuses to meet my eye, and his friends follow suit.

Suddenly, I feel drained. If there's any chance of us winning in Delhi, it'll take all of us together. I just don't know how I can get them to trust me.

The next day at practice, it's more of the same. Nothing I say to Ashok or his friends seems to get through to them. They will not cooperate. I know that they have skills to bring to the game, but for two days in a row they refuse to use them. Would Ashok really risk his own position on the team to get me kicked off as captain? Would he really resort to sabotage?

Then, as I walk past Ashok, he hisses something at me under his breath.

I can't make out what it is, but I know it's bad just by the menace on his face.

I'm not scared of him, I tell myself. *I'm the captain.*

I stop, turn around, and look him in the eye. "What's your problem with me?" I ask.

"Your parents aren't legally married," he says calmly. "Sikhs and Muslims can't marry."

My fists form an automatic ball. "Yes, they can. This is India," I reply. I feel ready to punch him, but I refrain. He's on my team. If I fight him, I can't lead him.

"Your mother isn't a real Indian. Her country is Pakistan. You all should just go there," Ashok says.

I can't tell if the dull roar I hear is a plane flying or if it's coming from inside my head. "I'm as Indian as you. My mother can trace her family back seven generations in this town," I say, my voice getting louder. But then I imagine Coach telling me to keep a level head.

I scan Ashok's face. He's eager for a fight, glad that my voice is rising. His eyes look hungry for it.

I won't give him the satisfaction.

I toss my braid behind my shoulders, sniff, and walk away. Only then do I notice Coach watching the exchange.

⁂

"Simi, stay for a few minutes," Coach says after practice the next day.

The field around us slowly empties. After a stretch of quiet, interrupted only by the rustling of leaves and distant shouts from the departing team, Coach finally breaks the silence.

"I want you to know you're not alone in this," Coach says, his voice steady but concerned.

"I can see how the team interacts, and I've heard a few whispers here and there."

I nod, my grip tightening around the stick in my hand.

"It's never easy being in the shoes of a captain," he continues. "And on top of that, you're dealing with so much more than you should have to. But you have the team behind you—well, most of them—and you definitely have me. We're going to work on this, together."

I let out a slow breath, feeling the warm air leave my lungs. "It feels like no matter what I do, it's never about how I play. It's about who I am, where I come from."

"That's a tough burden to bear," he says. "But remember, it's not just about proving them wrong. It's about proving to yourself that you can rise above it, that you are more than their narrow views."

I feel a mixture of relief and determination. "I'm not ready to give up," I say. "I'll keep trying."

"Good." He smiles. "Because being captain isn't just about leading the ones who are easy to lead. It's also about winning over the tough ones, like Ashok. You don't have to do it alone, but you do need to show them why you're the captain."

I think about his words, about Ashok's sneers and the team's hesitant glances. "I'll try," I say. "Maybe it's about finding the right moment, the right play."

"Exactly." Coach nods. "Use your skills, your understanding of the game. Let your leadership on the field speak for itself. They'll come around. You'll see."

Day after day, Ashok does nothing but ignore me and hang back during practice—his effort minimal, his body language closed off. So I grant Ashok his wish. I decide to leave him alone.

But deep down, I know how badly he really wants to play.

I watch him fiddle with the wrap around his hockey stick, thinking that he's trying to make a point by not playing the sport he clearly loves. I watch him get antsier and antsier. And then, as the first practice of the following week rolls around, I decide to try to show him what he's missing, by giving him a chance.

"Ashok," I call during a lull in the action. He looks surprised to hear his name. "We need you on defense," I instruct. "You know what to do. Anticipate their moves, cut off their angles." The challenge in my voice was clear: *Be a part of this, or step aside.*

His eyes meet mine, and he takes my advice. It's a gamble, but to my surprise, it works. After the play is over, Ashok looks back at me. His eyes meet mine before he gives me a nod.

As the days go by, I can feel my team's faith in me growing. I can feel myself running the next leg of the race after Abbu.

But of all the small wins so far, Ashok's nod has felt the biggest.

CHAPTER FOUR

By the middle of the following week, the window has been repaired and no one has mentioned COMBAM in days. Each morning, Abbu makes me eggs, I make Ammi tea. They ask about my courses and hockey. They go to work. I go to school. At practice, I keep Coach's advice in my head and try to let my knowledge of the game speak for itself.

But when I return home from practice on Wednesday, there are papers scattered across our doorstep. They're pamphlets—ugly, mean ones that say all sorts of things about Muslims.

Some of the pamphlets have the name of a political party—the Brotherhood for Justice—who talk just like the COMBAM crowd. Ammi and Abbu refer to them as the "Brotherhood for Just Bigots Party."

We should have one god, one religion, one language, one food, one dress . . . one, one, one . . . their spokespeople often say on TV. *Only oneness will bring efficiency to our country.*

"Idiots," Abbu always sighs. "India's unity is in its diversity. Our productivity comes from a chemistry of all our differences."

On our doorstep, Dadu doesn't waste a second. He grabs the pamphlets, his face burning with anger, and flings them straight into the trash.

"As usual, all their facts are wrong," he fumes. "Just a bunch of ignorant people!"

But just as he finishes his rant and I sit down to do my homework in the kitchen, a knock sounds at the door. Dadu, Dadi, and I stop and stare, wondering who's on the other side this time. Three men stand in our doorway. One of them is the squat little man who's always lingering near the betel shop on our lane. He stinks of sweat.

Dadi looks scared, but she opens the door and takes them to the living room. I catch a glimpse of them settling down comfortably in our armchairs. My kitchen table is a good vantage point to overhear everything without being assaulted by the stink.

But then Dadi firmly shuts the door between the kitchen and the living room. I feel a shiver go down my spine. I hear some words drift through the French window.

". . . so there is no beef in your fridge?" someone is asking.

But the answer fades away.

Their questions keep coming, but I can't make out their words.

I feel my heart press painfully against my ribs. Why is this happening? When will it end? I pray that Ammi doesn't walk in. Finally, after fifteen minutes or so, they walk out toward the driveway through the French doors. The square-jawed one, their leader, bends over and spits into one of our flowerpots of delicate ferns.

I walk into the living room and perch myself on the handle of Dadu's armchair.

"What did they want?" I ask.

"They want to know if a Muslim lives in the house," Dadu says calmly, as if it's not something I should be worried about. "They asked if we had beef in the fridge. They don't want us to eat beef because in Hinduism, the cow is considered sacred."

I think of a future without Nani's succulent kebabs. But I realize that there are far bigger problems. My heart is hammering. They came to find out if Ammi was living here. What does this mean? I clench my teeth against the bitter taste in my throat.

"What do they plan on doing?" I ask, my voice a little squeaky.

"They just like to disrupt our family life. These people have nothing better to do," grumbles Dadu.

But as I look at Dadi, I can see the concern grow across her face.

I hear Ammi's and Abbu's footsteps on the driveway

then. I get up and open the door, pulling out the pamphlets from the trash can as Dadu and Dadi talk about the visit by the men.

Ammi cooks silently as we huddle around the kitchen table. Dinner is a quiet event.

"Eat quickly, Simi," Ammi says. "I want you to get into bed early. You need plenty of rest, what with hockey practice before classes . . ."

I have a feeling she wants me out of the way so that the grown-ups can discuss everything without alarming me.

"Alright." I nod as I gulp down the food. Soon I am tucked in bed with a book. Ammi comes in and give me a good-night kiss. But a few minutes after she leaves, I get up and open my bedroom door slightly.

Ammi's footsteps become softer as she walks across the Kashmiri silk carpet in the hallway. My parents bought it on their honeymoon in Srinagar. It has flowers and leaves and birds in pastel colors of blue, pink, green, and red.

I hear the clatter of teacups and someone handing out chai.

Then Dadu speaks. "Things are only going to get worse now that those COMBAM people have the backing of the Brotherhood party. You, Henna, and Simi are growing targets." He takes a deep breath. "I think that you both should seriously consider leaving this country with Simi."

I hold my breath and move closer to the door. A light streaks down the dark corridor toward my room. I can see the shadows of the trees on the wall.

"Go where? Do what?" my abbu asks.

The wind rustles outside.

"Your cousin Kuldeep works for a taxi company in New York. He can help you settle in," says Dadi.

I clasp my hand over my mouth. How could Dadi agree with Dadu's wild plan?

There is a heavy silence while I wait for either Abbu or Ammi to respond.

"That's out of the question," Abbu finally declares. "We are not going anywhere."

There is silence until I can only hear Dadi's cane as she walks to the living room. I hear her open the lid of the gramophone.

Malika Pukhraj's throaty voice fills the room with songs of love.

I breathe again.

The next day after school, instead of going home, I go to the place that I've always thought of as my safe haven. Nanaji and Nani's library is lined with floor-to-ceiling bookcases. Nanaji sits in the rocking chair by the window with a half-opened newspaper. I pause for a moment to take it in. For a moment it feels like nothing in the world has changed or ever will.

But no matter how hard I try, I can't get Dadu's words out of my head. *I think that you both should seriously consider leaving this country with Simi.*

Nanaji looks up with a smile and cocks an eyebrow. "Why are you dawdling near the door? Come give me a hug."

All I want is for Nanaji to pull out a book that will have an answer.

I run in, enfold him in a warm hug, and plonk down on the armchair nearby. Nani walks in with a plate laden with sponge cake. I bite into the crust of my cake as Nanaji glances over from his newspaper. "How was school today?" he asks with a soft smile.

"Same old, same old, Nanaji. Nothing special." I try to sound casual, but I can't hide anything from him. He sets his newspaper aside, leans forward, polishing his glasses, and peers at me with concern. Nervously, I blurt out, "Do marriages between Sikhs and Muslims not count? Like Ammi and Abbu's marriage?"

Nanaji straightens, pushing his glasses back up his nose with a frown. "Of course their marriage counts."

I sigh, feeling a mix of frustration and confusion. "I know that. I do. But then why would anyone believe otherwise?"

He scowls deeper, shaking his head. "They're wrong. They obviously don't know the law."

"But how do you tell someone they're wrong when they believe the complete opposite? And when they're so angry about it? I wouldn't even know how to begin," I admit, feeling overwhelmed. "How long do I have to wait until things change back to normal?"

Nanaji slides his glasses up to his forehead, his eyes meeting mine intently. "Getting people to understand someone else's beliefs or point of view can be challenging. But it doesn't have to be a waiting game. It's crucial to act, and important to remember that every action we take sends a ripple through the world." He leans a bit closer, his voice earnest. "It's important to act with kindness and respect, so that we spread those qualities instead of more hate and anger."

"How?" I ask impatiently.

Nanaji takes a moment, his eyes thoughtful. "You're a leader, aren't you? A captain? Gandhiji believed that 'you must be the change you wish to see in the world.' You must set an example and show others a path they might follow. If we want a world of understanding and respect, especially between people of different faiths, that's how we must act ourselves." He pauses, ensuring I'm following along. "Our methods—how we conduct ourselves—are a reflection of the change itself. The *way* we fight for something can be just as important as what we are fighting for."

Nani, who had been listening quietly, adds her wisdom. "You have to be prepared to defend your beliefs, Simi. But remember, if we act with integrity and love, then we are already fostering the world we want to live in."

I think about what Coach had said about how it's just as important to win over the tough ones, like Ashok. About how I'm more than their narrow views. And then I think of my interaction with Ashok from earlier this week, when he finally listened to me. Ashok and his friends still play rough. They might only listen to half the things I say. They may not like me, but they no longer ignore me. Change is slow, but I can feel it happening.

Nani takes my hands in hers, her eyes full of understanding. "Simi, whenever a negative thought enters your mind, try to replace it with a positive one. If a hateful thought arises, think instead of what you love. So, when you see those combative people or anyone from that Bigot Party," Nani said, "think of something delightful. Something like . . . sheekh kebab."

She smiles, her eyes twinkling with a mix of mischief and wisdom.

CHAPTER FIVE

I spend the entire weekend mulling over Nanaji's advice. How do you defend yourself with love? How do I stop these men from knocking on our door and going through our food with just love? How can I possibly protect Ammi with just love?

I try to think of something pleasant—like Nani suggested.

"Sheekh kebab," I repeat to myself. Surprisingly, the mental image of those kebabs fills my senses so vividly that I become more hungry than worried. But the problem remains.

And then on Monday, as I approach the school gate, I see two men distributing flyers. I recognize them immediately. I can still see the image of them in our living room—the squat, little one who stinks of sweat and the big, aggressive one who spat into the pot of ferns.

I read the bold print across the top of a flyer: PRESERVE PURE INDIAN GENES.

My fists clench as I imagine ways to retaliate. I now recognize the taller one as the builder at the construction site down the road. My stomach knots with anger, the memories of their intrusion still fresh.

I close my eyes and try to remember Nanaji's and Nani's words. That it takes time for things to change, but it doesn't have to be a waiting game.

When I open my eyes, the man is still there, but I try to breathe. I feel calmer, more in control of my emotions.

Ravi appears and sees me looking at the man with the flyers. He flinches in disgust. "What if we puncture their car tires? The shorter one with the belly—he always parks near the betel shop."

I shake my head. "That would only reinforce their beliefs against us," I reply. "But we'll think of something. Something that would set a good example."

Ravi gives me a look that suggests the idea feels impossible.

The school bell's clang reverberates through the crowded halls as we dodge our way around the throng of students. Ashok and his friends wear smirks on their faces as they pass us, and then Ashok's eyes flick to mine. For a moment it feels like the expression on his face is guilt. And then I see them—the rolled-up flyers that the men were passing out wedged into his back pocket—and my breath stops.

For some reason, even after everything Ashok has said to me, it still feels like a shock.

How could I have begun to think that Ashok had started to change? How could I have thought that one nod from him meant he accepted me?

"Sheekh kebab," I whisper to myself.

Sheekh kebab. Sheekh kebab.

This time, it doesn't work.

"Do these people know that most Muslims in India are farmers and artisans?" Ravi says, adjusting his glasses like he always does when he's about to share some big fact. "You know, like weavers and embroiderers—people who make beautiful stuff by hand. India's crafts are, like, our biggest export! And get this—the sitar and the samosa? They actually came from Muslim countries!"

After I floated the idea this morning, he's been trying to think of peaceful ways to get these men to stop their antics. But ever since seeing Ashok with those flyers, my mind has been elsewhere.

Reena's eyes widen in excitement. "What if we made our own flyer with written facts about Muslims?"

"They'd probably just crush it and throw it away," I respond wryly. What does Ashok even plan to do with that garbage? Is he just going to turn into one of *them*?

Reena and Ravi both turn to me, surprised by my rare moment of negativity, I assume.

I know that Nani and Nanaji are right. That Coach is right.

I am surrounded by good advice, but why is it that it's so hard to put good advice into practice when it matters most?

It's about proving to yourself that you can rise above it.

Be the change you wish to see.

Think instead of what you love.

I think of Ammi watering her flowers, Abbu stirring our tea. I imagine Abbu's tea leaves falling to the bottom of his porcelain china cup and seeing a future where the change has already happened. There are no pamphlets or men knocking on our door or rocks thrown through our window. I tell myself that this day will come.

I sit up, resolving not to give up.

As the final bell rings, I shake off the heavy air of the classroom and grab my hockey stick, eager for the open space of the field, the scent of fresh-cut grass, and the sunlight that weaves gold into the green expanse ahead.

"Let's pair up!" I call, the sound slicing through the chatter. The team shuffles, forming pairs. I stride over to

Ashok. "You're with me," I announce, steeling myself for the challenge.

We begin with passes, the ball thumping against our sticks. Ashok's friends line up along the sidelines, their chuckles forming a mocking chorus. "Watch him take her down," one jeers, nudging another.

Unexpectedly, Ashok whips a pass at me—too sharp, a clear attempt to throw me off. But I trap it smoothly, my return pass snapping back to him with precision. "Nice!" I say, pretending his trick was a real attempt. "Now, try adding a bit more arc," I instruct. I demonstrate with a fluid motion of my stick. Ashok tries. The ball arcs beautifully from his stick back to mine, tracing a perfect path under the azure sky.

"That's it! Precision, not power," I call out, ensuring his friends hear the praise. Their laughter dwindles, replaced by murmurs of surprise.

For the rest of the scrimmage, I decide to keep Ashok involved, calling plays that showcase his skills. I call for him to go left and he does. The ball meets his stick, and he drives it home. "Great shot!" I yell.

After practice, as we collect the scattered cones and balls, I approach him, a friendly nudge accompanying my smile. "You were really in the zone today."

He hesitates, his usual scowl softening as he meets my gaze. "Yeah, thanks for the tips," he mutters, his voice almost drowned by the distant shouts from the soccer field.

His friends, still clutching their sticks, look on in baffled silence, their expectations of conflict unmet. One prods Ashok, whispering something I can't hear, but Ashok just shrugs, his earlier attitude cooled, if only slightly.

I walk away from the field, the background noise fading into a comforting buzz. My heart feels lighter, hopeful after the shared sweat of a successful practice.

The next morning, I pull Ravi and Reena aside before math.

"Remember what you said about samosas coming from Muslim countries?" I say.

"Yeah?" Ravi responds, curious.

"That halwai who makes those amazing jalebis near our lane told me his syrup recipe has been passed down from his Arab ancestors for over seven generations," I share excitedly.

"And?" Reena presses.

"And we're going to order samosas and jalebis from him and have them delivered to that builder and his crew at their construction site," I explain. "The ones who were handing out flyers yesterday."

Reena looks puzzled. "Because you want to kill them with sweets?"

I chuckle softly. "Because it's a kind gesture."

"Why do they deserve our kindness?" Ravi retorts.

I think about what Nanaji might say. "Because everyone does. And if we set a good example, maybe they'll follow."

Ravi and Reena exchange a look.

"Then we'll need to print that flyer after all," Ravi says finally, his eyes lighting up.

As soon as school lets out, we linger near the halwai

shop, soaking in the aroma of spiced potatoes frying.

We place our order and follow the delivery boy to the building site.

We watch from a distance as the men dig into the samosas and jalebis, sprawling on plastic chairs amid their construction chaos. After giving them ten minutes to enjoy the snacks, we approach.

Their frowns deepen at our interruption.

"Namaste, Uncle," I greet them politely. "I hope you enjoyed the samosas."

"What do you want?" the tall one snaps back.

Ravi steps forward and hands them the flyers:

These snacks were made by an Indian Muslim, and the recipes are from Muslim countries. Please enjoy them and remember: Our culture is richer because of its variety. You would never have had the chance to enjoy a samosa or a jalebi if it weren't for Muslim contributions to our country.

The squat guy gapes, a half-eaten samosa in his hands.

The builder's eyes bulge as he quickly chomps down on

the samosa already in his mouth. "Get lost, you imps!" he yells.

"Thank you for thanking us for the food you are eating," says Reena.

We chorus "Namaste" and turn to leave, our heads held high while they look openmouthedly at us.

Outside we three grin from ear to ear and high-five.

I ride my bike home, cutting through the breeze.

I park my bicycle near the kitchen garden and am walking into the house when I see Dadi sitting on a cane stool on the porch.

My heart sinks. Something feels wrong.

"Where is everybody, Dadi? Are you crying?" I ask.

It takes a little more time for Dadi to calm down before she is able to reply.

"Your abbu was attacked."

CHAPTER SIX

My heart is trembling.

My voice is shaking.

"What happened? Where was he attacked? Was he alone? Will he be okay?" I ask.

All Dadi can say at first is that Abbu's knees are hurt.

Eventually, I learn that four men with COMBAM headbands had blocked the isolated farm road when Abbu was returning home on his motorcycle. He swerved, lost control, and crashed to the ground, where the men beat him badly.

They smashed his knees. If it hadn't been for the

farmworkers who rescued him, Abbu would have lain there for hours. Now he's at the hospital with Ammi and Dadu.

I go inside, slosh some cold water from the kitchen sink on my face and arms, and try to distract myself while we wait for more news. I put the kettle on and make Dadi lie down on the sofa near the phone. I switch on the TV to distract her from worrying. I bring out my schoolbooks and spread them on the dining table.

Studying will stop me from thinking about Abbu.

Every second of today comes to my mind—the samosas, the feeling of joy I had only a moment ago. But it's all gone now. Everything has changed in an instant.

Dadi lights a candle and puts it in front of the little Ganesh statue in the kitchen. I put my books away and go to my secret corner in the garden. We both need to be alone.

Finally, I let go of myself.

I sob and sob and sob till nothing is left inside me. The emptiness brings a sense of calm.

I heat the food, serve it to Dadi and myself. Both of

us toy with our helpings, each eating for the sake of the other.

Finally, the front door creaks open and Ammi and Dadu walk inside.

Ammi pulls me to her and kisses me on the head. Dadu holds Dadi tight and whispers again and again, "He's okay, he's okay." They barely touch the food that Dadi and I insist they eat. Ammi's roti has become hard. I get her a glass of warm milk.

She shakes her head. "I don't need it."

"Yes, you do, you have to keep your strength up to look after Gurbeer," says Dadi firmly.

Ammi sips the milk absentmindedly, a tiny smile at the end of her lips, in acknowledgment of our care.

I cuddle into Ammi as the three adults talk and shuffle papers around. Words like *mortgage* and *bank-owned* float around me. I don't catch everything, but the gist is clear enough: Abbu can't work with his wrecked knees, and his surgery is going to cost a fortune. We're going to have to give up the farm, or at least a big chunk of it, to cover the costs.

I had been so happy this afternoon; the day had felt triumphant. Now, as I see Ammi's face tighten and Dadu's hands shake as he sorts through the papers, I feel the enormity of what has happened. That farm is my favorite place; it's where I've played in the fields every summer since I was little. Thinking about losing it makes my chest hurt.

The clock strikes eleven, and Dadu gets up wearily to switch off the light.

It's raining the next morning, so I can't see out of the window. Ammi is already bathed and ready in her starched, white cotton nurse uniform, her hair neatly tucked under her nurse's cap, as if everything is normal.

It's like any other day, but for me, everything has changed. This morning, there's no aroma of freshly cooked food or the clinking sounds of Ammi or Dadi packing my tiffin. Instead, I find myself wrapping up some snacks in newspaper—two bundles, one for Ammi and one for me. It's a small act, me taking care of things, but it feels like I'm growing up fast.

She brings out my raincoat to keep my dress from getting wet.

"Will you call me if something happens?" I ask Ammi when we reach the school gate.

"Yes, darling, soon as surgery is over, I'll phone the headmistress."

"You promise?" I ask. There are tears in my eyes. She kisses me three or four times, straightens the nurse's cap on her head, and waves as she cycles off.

"Don't forget to eat," I remind her, saying what she so often says to me.

My heart feels like it's in a python's grip. School is a hazy blur. Ravi takes notes for a change while my mind keeps wandering to the hospital. I wonder if our message of nonviolence to those COMBAM men at the construction site even scratched the surface. Such a tiny thing. Maybe it was too tiny. Maybe trying to change minds with kindness and food is like trying to stop a tsunami with an umbrella. But then I think about how we left—with our dignity, not letting their hate win. Maybe it wasn't about changing those men's minds. Maybe it was about proving to ourselves that we can face hate without becoming hateful.

The teacher slips me a note at some point to say the surgery is over. That my dad is okay.

The tightness around my heart uncoils and tears prick my eyes.

In this whirlwind of a day, I feel older, somehow.

I get into bed with Ammi that night. The wind has begun to rise, and our old watering can rattles down the garden path. She pulls me into her as we tuck the blanket a little tighter around us.

I squeeze Ammi's hand, seeking comfort in her presence.

"Are you asleep?" I whisper.

"No, not really," she responds softly.

"He's not going to die?" I ask her, pleading.

"Of course not. His legs are not as badly injured as they had originally thought. He will be okay, especially now that he's successfully had his operation." Ammi's tone is calmer, more reassured than outside the school gates this morning.

Her words help a little, but as I snuggle closer, matching my breathing with hers, I can't shake the feeling that everything is about to change even more than it already has. And not just at home. I can feel it everywhere, like a storm about to break. Those COMBAM men are part of something bigger, something meaner, and I don't know if there are enough samosas and jalebis in the world to change their minds before they strike again. I wish more than anything that my worries were about our hockey competition in Delhi, or what I should wear to the end-of-school dance, or getting a high enough score on the next math quiz. But suddenly, all of those things feel smaller and smaller as the hours go by since Abbu was attacked.

As I snuggle closer to Ammi, I know deep down that there are a lot of things we can't be ready for, no matter how much we want to be.

I try to think about something positive. *Sheekh kebab. Ammi, and Abbu, and Nanaji and Nani, and Dadu and Dadi.*

Our family is so full of love.

I'm so scared about what might happen, but having them near me makes everything seem easier.

When I turn to my right side, Ammi turns too. My body relaxes.

We mold into each other and fall asleep, her hair falling on me.

Everything is different, but she's still here.

CHAPTER SEVEN

Over the course of the next few weeks, our living room becomes the center of our world.

Abbu isn't supposed to be on his feet for a month, and after that, he's only allowed limited steps until the physical therapist approves more.

I spend my afternoons with my schoolbooks spread across the carpet. Abbu spends his days poring over the account books. It's strange seeing him so fragile, lounging on his daybed by the window. Dadi and Dadu strategize over their chessboard. Ammi, nearby, stitches colorful patterns onto old fabrics, giving them new life.

Ammi's taken on extra shifts at the hospital, and it shows. The spark in her eyes dims with each passing day, and our meals have grown simpler—leftovers remade, and treats a rare luxury.

It's always a struggle for Abbu to keep up with his account books. He doesn't have a head for numbers, but he keeps at it, in case he can find a way to save some money.

Abbu looks up and smiles at me. I am caught in the warm glow of his eyes.

"Want me to help?" I say, sliding in next to him.

"Thank you," Abbu says gratefully.

I quickly reconcile the monthly expenses with the earnings and show him how much is left over. The cabbage, onion, and wheat sales are in one column. The seed and fertilizer purchase is in another, along with labor costs and utilities. I total each column, subtract one from the other, and show him how much he has in hand. "There it is, Abbu. This is your profit," I say, sliding the book to him.

My father rolls his eyes, grins, and says, "My daughter is both smart and athletic, unlike her old man."

Every morning and every day after school, I take any energy that I have and leave it on the hockey field. Each time I pick up my hockey stick, it feels like I'm picking up a baton that Abbu has handed off to me.

One sunny afternoon, Dadi and I visit the farm. My feet sink slightly into the soft earth, a familiar comfort. I trace my hands over the rough bark of the guava tree, our loyal watchman. The farm misses Abbu as much as we do. Weeds have crept over the edges of the fields, and the fences sag, needing repair. The serenity of the land clashes with the harsh reality of our finances.

The day our electricity is cut off marks a low point.

That night, candlelight flickers across our faces as we sit around the kitchen table, the unpaid bills casting long shadows.

The air grows heavy with the weight of decisions.

Dadi sells a gold necklace to tide us over a few months.

Nanaji and Nani visit more often, their faces etched with worry. Each knock on the door brings anxious whispers about the Brotherhood for Justice, whose signs and slogans are becoming more common in town.

Nanaji's voice shakes as he talks about their growing popularity. "It's not just about politics. It's about our way of life being threatened," he says, looking over his shoulder as if they might be listening. There are more and more stories about families like us—families who have been attacked, even arrested. Doors that have been plastered with pamphlets. Messages that have been delivered to their doorsteps, telling them to leave again and again. Outside, the banners of the Brotherhood for Justice flutter ominously. Their rallies fill the streets with angry voices and stern faces. The sound seeps through our walls, spoiling the brief moments of peace we find. More and more of our practices have been canceled because of nearby protests. Even Nanaji begins to whisper about the option for us to move to the US.

In this shrinking world of ours, we pull closer together in the evenings.

Stories are told, games are played, laughter is shared.

Our living room, with its patchwork of family and memories, becomes a fortress against the uncertainty outside. Here, in the soft glow of candles and the warmth of my family, I find the strength to face another day.

Tonight, the couches and chairs are pulled close, making our little circle even tighter.

The decision looming over us is getting too big to ignore.

I sit, tucked between Ammi and Nanaji. The weight of the conversation presses down like a brick on me. Money is tighter than ever. But if Abbu moves to the US and earns enough money, maybe, just maybe, he can pull us back from the brink and save our farm.

"What about everything Abbu will miss out on here?" I ask, the words tumbling out. "Like Nani's birthday, and all my matches? And just . . . everyday stuff?" *What about the championship match in Delhi?* I think to myself. There is no one who I care more about being there than Abbu. So that he can see I'm picking up where he left off.

Nanaji's face softens as he looks at me, understanding

my fears. "Of course, you and your mother will go with him. That way, he won't have to miss those precious moments."

My heart sinks.

Ammi looks worriedly at the ground, then back up at us. "The costs of moving Gurbeer alone are daunting—visas, plane tickets . . . and it's expensive there. Without me being able to work as a nurse right away, how will we manage?"

Nani squeezes Ammi's hand.

"Nani, what about you and Nanaji? Dadi and Dadu?" I manage to say, holding back a sob.

"Parmeshwar tuhāḍē nāla, God is with you." Nani's voice is a steady comfort as she trots out her favorite phrase. "One thing at a time. Let your abbu go first, set things up. Once he's settled, you and your ammi will follow. And we'll keep things together here so that by the time you return, things will be just as you left them."

Abbu sighs deeply, a sound of a man burdened by too much. "I want to fight here, stay here. This is our country, our home," he says stubbornly, but his eyes dart around the room until he finds Ammi. "But home will follow us wherever we are."

Dadu, always the peacemaker, adds softly, "Come back to your farm when the times change, son. We'll be here waiting for you."

The room falls silent.

We all cling a bit closer. Amid the fear and the plans, we brace for whatever comes next, knowing that no matter how far apart we might end up, our little circle will keep us connected.

After that night, everything speeds up so fast. We barely have time to breathe.

Ammi is glued to the phone, talking tickets and passports. Abbu reviews documents over and over, and I try to catch every word, hoping for good news. The elections are just around the corner, and every day the news is full of stories about the Brotherhood for Justice party gaining more support.

What will happen if they win? What happens to families like ours? To Nanaji and Nani? But also, I secretly hope, what will happen if they lose? What if it becomes safe enough for Abbu, all of us, to stay right where we are?

Then, one afternoon, right as we step through the door, Ammi hangs up the phone, her face clouded with disappointment. "The travel agent just called. The US denied your abbu's visa application."

My heart leaps—surprisingly, I'm happy. Maybe this means we can stay together!

Abbu exhales deeply and tries to joke. "The US doesn't need hockey players or farmers from India, I guess."

But the relief doesn't last long. Nanaji, always the one to see the big picture, cuts straight to the heart of it. "Attackers are targeting interfaith couples all over the country," he says grimly. "Now they're even getting the police on their side, breaking up interfaith marriages before they happen. This is not just about your finances." For a moment, Nanaji's eyes flick to me, and Abbu's and Ammi's eyes follow. "You must leave quickly, visa or no visa."

The bubble of joy in my chest bursts.

The house feels colder, tenser. If the Brotherhood for Justice could hurt Abbu in broad daylight before, what would they be capable of if they win the election? Guilt gnaws at me for wanting him to stay. The fear that had started to ebb comes rushing back in a fierce tide.

I look around our living room, at the walls lined with family photos, at Ammi's plants crowding the windowsill, at Abbu's old hockey stick propped in the corner. This is our home. How can we just leave it all behind?

"How would I get to the US with no visa?" Abbu asks Nanaji. There is a new determination in his voice.

"There are other ways. I am sure your travel agent knows of the Donkey Express," Nanaji replies. "They are chartered planes that smuggle Punjabis to America illegally. There is no other option, Gurbeer. You will have to pay a smuggler."

I keep my head down and squeeze my eyelids together so tight that it hurts. I see the shadows of the trees change into ominous shapes of unknown monsters. My heart sinks. My throat tightens. Abbu will go away. The person who makes the best omelets, who teaches me to drive the tractor and play hockey, will live somewhere else. How will he keep his accounts without me?

When I open my eyes again, everyone I love around me is nodding solemnly in agreement.

This is happening, and it's happening soon.

Three days and many hushed phone calls later, Ammi announces that not only is Abbu leaving, but he has a way out—via Mexico. *A way out*. How has our life come to this? Our beautiful little life. There is a mix of relief and worry in Ammi's voice. The plan is detailed and daunting: Abbu will fly to Mexico through Spain, and from there, smugglers will help him cross into the US.

It sounds like something out of a spy movie, not our lives. Abbu's cousin will meet him on the other side and drive him to Queens, New York. The cost is staggering—nearly three million rupees, nearly everything we have.

Despite all the plans, there is a part of me that secretly

wishes that something will change soon—that the situation here will get better. That good people will prevail and I can go back to worrying about Ashok not listening to me on the field. Not the idea of Abbu sneaking around like a fugitive. I hide these thoughts, though, afraid to say them out loud because they seem as flimsy as air.

At school, I find myself looking up Mexico on the computer during my free period. It's a world away from here, with ancient pyramids and traditions stretching back centuries, almost like a mirror reflecting our own rich culture.

I click through photos of New York, with its towering skyscrapers and the Statue of Liberty shining like a beacon. It looks dazzling, so different from anything I've ever known.

Ravi and Reena catch me staring at the screen. "Planning a vacation?" Ravi jokes, nudging me. And I realize I have to tell them. I can't keep putting it off.

The lump in my throat wobbles. Everything comes out. The plan for Abbu. The expectation that Ammi and I will follow once he's settled. "Nobody can know that

Abbu is leaving for America," I say once it's all out. "If anyone asks about him, just say that he is still resting in bed at home. That he is still recovering from his surgery." My faltering smile hides the heaviness in my chest.

Reena's expression falls. "America is so far, Simi. Are you okay with this?"

I nod, but my throat feels tight. "I have to be, right? Once he's settled, he'll send for us. So we won't have to do it illegally. I'm trying to think of it all as an adventure."

Ravi looks skeptical, and under that I can see his sadness. I recognize it instantly. He looks exactly how I feel. "It sounds scary to me. Going all that way, and sneaking across borders?" Ravi says. "Aren't you scared for him?"

I shrug, trying to seem braver than I feel. "A little. But we don't have much choice. Things here . . ." My voice trails off, and I glance away, feeling that familiar prick of tears.

Reena gives my hand a quick squeeze. "It'll be okay, Simi. It has to."

Ravi looks at me, his eyes glassy. "You'll be okay. And then you'll come back home and everything will be like normal," he says, but I can tell he doesn't believe it.

Their words are meant to comfort, but a knot of worry settles in my stomach.

I'm scared for Abbu. Scared for all of us. The whole plan feels like a house of cards, ready to collapse at the slightest touch. But it's the only plan we have.

CHAPTER EIGHT

It's Saturday, the day before Abbu is scheduled to leave for Mexico and on to America.

I wake early and walk the familiar steps to the kitchen. Abbu hands me a plate with a poached egg, just like it's any other day. Ammi pulls out her crossword.

The familiar sounds of the house fill the room. The morning news from the TV in Dadu's room, water running in Dadi's bathroom, the rustle of leaves in the mango tree at the end of the garden, the gentle spring breeze through the French windows. The fruit-cart vendor cycles by in his cart, calling out the name of each fruit. A cat streaks across the yard.

"Shall we arrange some flowers this morning?" Ammi asks. "The forget-me-nots and roses will look nice in the living room. They're in full bloom."

We go outside—Ammi, and Abbu, and I. It feels like a gift to be able to see Abbu walking again.

I carefully cut the branches, making sure they are long enough to put in a vase. A patch of sunshine falls on Ammi. Abbu takes a front-row seat as we spread a newspaper sheet on the table in the garden. Ammi pulls out a crystal vase and a red bowl. I pour water into the two while Ammi cuts the flowers. She arranges them at different angles, adds in a few pebbles to hold them, and sends me out for a few leaves. As she adds the finishing touches, the flowers seem to get bigger and brighter, right in front of my eyes.

"Simi," Abbu says. "When you and Ammi are done, would you like to come for a picnic at the farm with me?"

"I would love to," I say, trying not to think beyond this moment.

Because at this moment, all is well in the world.

FEAR AND FLIGHT

Abbu and I stand near the gate to the farm, looking across the fields. I feel as I always do when we go to the farm, a rush of freedom and happiness. Gooseberry and mango trees border our fields, their tops waving in the sun. Birds twitter. Wildflowers circle the roots of the trees that flutter in the gentle noonday breeze. A covey of geese flies overhead, screaming as they pass over the stone shed.

We cross to the lower end of our farm toward the pond. The tiny path of pebbles that leads to it is crowded with young ferns and stalks of water chestnut, sponge plants, cowslips, and water dragons. Under these, hidden among the leaves and thorns, are speckled thousands of wildflowers, beautiful and precious in their tininess.

At last, Abbu and I reach the ancient peepal fig tree and settle on two low rocks, surrounded by ferns. It is mine and Abbu's secret place. We have been sitting on these rocks for my entire life, watching the tadpoles play in the little pool in between.

The big pond reflects the naked blue of the sky above. There is not a ripple in it. I pick up a pebble and give it a toss toward the water. It skims effortlessly seven times. Abbu, my pebble-throwing teacher, smiles proudly. "I taught you that."

At last, I ask the question that has been on my mind for weeks. "Are you afraid?"

He looks at me intently through his brown, affectionate eyes. "Afraid of what?" I know his face by heart. A pleasant, full face, bushy black eyebrows, a jaw that sometimes twitches, a beard, and a turban.

"That something will happen to you," I say quickly, and when I have said it, I start to shiver. But there are so many ways to answer that question. So many things to be fearful of: of going to a different country. Of Abbu illegally crossing the border into the US. Of anything and everything that could go wrong. Of him being away from us.

"I'm not afraid. It's just a couple of hours of walking from the Mexico border to the US border. It's nothing for me." His voice is jovial at first, but I hold his stare until he gives me a real answer. "And because I know we will be together again soon. Once we're together, wherever we are, we'll be home."

I bow my head, believing and not believing him. "I wanted to take the team to Delhi," I say finally. "I wanted you to see me win."

Abbu raises his bushy eyebrows in a look of surprise. "I have seen you win in more ways than I'm able to count, Simi," he says. His eyes moisten. "You're already a bigger hockey champ than your old dad. You're a captain in everything you do."

Abbu puts his arm around my shoulders. I hold his hand. We stay like that, sharing this moment together. In an instant, my mood changes.

As we are leaving, a leaf floats down from the peepal tree. Abbu catches it. It's a delicate thing. The flesh has withered away, leaving behind a lacelike frame.

He gives it to me. "Look how nature has created this beautiful thing," Abbu says. "Keep it. See how even a flimsy leaf can outlast the seasons? We are humans. This too will pass."

FEAR AND FLIGHT

It is still dark the next morning when we take Abbu to the airport. There is hot tea and the potato parathas from last night's dinner for a quick breakfast. "How many hours is the flight?" Nanaji asks for the tenth time. Dadu again wants to know if Abbu has packed his passport and ticket carefully. I smile when they talk to him like he is twelve like me, and not a full-grown man.

We drive the six-hour journey from Punjab to the Delhi airport. I try not to think about how badly I'd wanted to take the team to Delhi for the gold cup. I never thought the road would lead me here to say goodbye to Abbu.

My nose stays glued to the window. We speed past little village schools just off the highway, temples and mosques, ponds and factories. Dadu sits in the front seat with the driver, Dadi and Abbu in the middle row, and Ammi and I in the back in the big Innova van—a six-seater with three rows of seats—that we have hired.

I nap on and off, lulled into sleep by the motion of the

car, stretched out on the back seat, my head in Ammi's lap, a shawl thrown over me.

The grown-ups talk, their words drifting in and out of my ears.

Soon, too soon, our van draws into the airport drop-off point. It's all glass and steel. I have never seen so much hurry in one place. It's hard to say goodbye in this crowded, anonymous setting. There is one round of hugs and then we hug once more. I take in Abbu's smell of coffee and freshly laundered cotton. I try to tell myself that he is just headed to the farm for the day. That he will come back home at dusk and everything will be normal again.

Tears run down Ammi's cheeks. Dadu's eyes glint with moisture too. Dadi whispers her beloved phrase, "Rabb tere te mehar kre, God be with you." She has her rosary out and is repeating, "Satnam, Satnam," with each bead. Abbu winks at me before walking toward the gate.

Together, we stand behind the iron rods as we watch Abbu disappear into the crowd.

CHAPTER NINE

It's been four days since Abbu has left and we are still waiting by the phone for him to call.

Ammi's mind is not with us.

I go to school as usual. Ammi goes to the hospital, Dadu to the farm, Nanaji to the clinic. Nani bakes. Dadi plays Bollywood songs. But a fear lingers in the air that we refuse to speak out loud.

At last, on the fifth day, we get the call.

"A man met me at the airport in a beat-up blue car," Abbu tells us. I have never been so happy to hear Abbu's voice. Ammi gets up and brings the teapot to the table. She pours herself, Dadi, and Dadu fresh cups with the utmost concentration. "He had my name on a big white sign and we drove to Mexicali, a small border town."

He tells us how the car shook violently the whole way. There were four other people with him. A family from Honduras. A husband, wife, and their two children. Abbu and the family did not know one another's language, but they were friendly. The same van that brought them from the airport took them to a remote area of the desert half an hour away. The driver told everyone to get out. Then he pointed toward a three-foot-high wall and told them to jump over it. "*Then keep walking. That is the US. When you see a border guard, just go surrender to him.*" Abbu's legs had gotten stronger every day and felt their strongest that day. He put on his sneakers, strapped his rucksack to his back, and jumped, bracing his sore knees for impact.

"And then nothing happened!" he says. "No one was there on the other side. Just a stretch of sand and a road in the distance."

And then he walked. The air was light and cool. Soon,

he could see signs in blue. Calexico. He was in the US.

Just like that.

The border guards saw him from their van and Abbu surrendered. He told them he wanted something called political asylum, which I've learned means "shelter."

I bite into my buttered toast as I listen. The room is silent.

They escorted Abbu to a facility that looked like a jail, took away all his things, and gave him a blue suit to wear. They even gave him a turban. He was there for three days. That's why he couldn't phone us.

"It took a couple more days for the paperwork, but now I am with my cousin Kuldeep," Abbu continues. "I will drive one of his taxis once I reach Queens and get a license. Kuldeep has even helped me find a lawyer in New York so we can be together very soon. Just as soon as I finish applying for your visas and get you political asylum."

We all breathe a collective sigh of relief.

Our family cannot thank all the gods enough for keeping Abbu safe. Dadu and Dadi take us to the community kitchen langar of the beautiful Sikh temple to make a donation as extra thanks. We all sit cross-legged on the floor to eat with the rest of the congregation. This is one of the traditions I love most about Sikhism. Everyone is fed free in the langar in the same way, regardless of caste, religion, social, or class status. No one is turned away.

We stop at the mosque on our way home. Ammi, Nani, Nanaji, and I go inside and thank Allah.

Dadu jokes as we drive home. "Simi is lucky. She has gods, goddesses, and prophets from three religions to look after her. More than most girls."

We talk to Abbu each night, which is morning for him in America. He has begun to drive Kuldeep's taxi at night. They have made a little apartment for him in their basement. It is very quiet there, and he can sleep peacefully even in the daytime. He's started saving money from the tips he earns driving the yellow cab and takes on odd jobs in his spare time. He mows lawns, paints fences, delivers boxes . . .

He tells Ammi that he has hired a lawyer in New York from one of those pro bono places, which I've learned means "free," and that we will be together very soon.

I cuddle into my bed with Ammi that night.

"Do you really think we will be with him soon?" I ask. I'm not sure what answer I'm looking for. I want Abbu to be here with us. But as the days go by leading up to the elections, it feels like everything's changing, and not in a good way. The country I've always known—the one that feels like home—is losing that safe, familiar feeling, like it's just slipping away.

Once we're together, wherever we are, we'll be home. I let Abbu's words fill my head.

"I think so," says Ammi, stroking my hair.

I close my eyes, and when I open them again Ammi is gone. At first I assume that it is morning until I notice that the room is still dark. There is a murmur of voices from the kitchen table, and I can hear my family stirring their tea. I lift my head and the room seems to move.

"So that's it. The Brotherhood has won . . ." Ammi says.

"They have enough votes to do what they want now," Dadu replies solemnly. "These people can attack us and get away with it."

There is a beat of silence.

"When is the soonest Gurbeer can get passports for you and Simi?" Dadi says at last.

I try to be brave. I try to think of something positive. But all I can think about is those gloating boys in brown shorts who called me Mozzy and their adult counterparts gobbling up our lives, gobbling up Ammi.

The forget-me-nots that Ammi put in a vase on my dresser are drooping. Nobody has replaced them for days. I pluck a dried flower and shred it petal by petal with my fingers.

Nanaji insists on driving me to school the next day. There are celebrations in the streets with the news of the elections. Throngs of supporters of the Brotherhood, of COMBAM, bang their drums and explode firecrackers.

There is song and dance along our lane while we and families like ours make sure our doors are locked tight.

It is like this for days, until the celebrations finally die down and I convince Nanaji to let me cycle to school like normal.

But school does not feel normal. There is a tension in the air that I have never felt before. As I move through the day, I hear whispers brushing against me like thorns. Though the murmurs are muted, I know they're flickering sparks about me—about my mixed-faith family.

I get out late from hockey practice. The sun has long slipped away as I ride home. The sky has turned purple. Our little lane is eerily empty. There are still the remnants of firecrackers in the streets. An old building groans in the wind, and some instinct sends a chill through my body. I hear the faint sound of whistling and instantly recognize the guttural melody as the song that the boys in the brown shorts sing.

Head down, I strain forward over my handlebars and pedal faster. My leg muscles burn. My heart beats furiously. I hear the slap of rubber slippers on the sidewalk.

There is a pack of them on bike and on foot—the boys in brown shorts. I pedal harder, sweating, hoping against hope that I reach my gate before them. But they are coming toward me from the jacaranda tree. I avert my gaze, focusing on my home.

They block my path. There are four of them.

One of them is Ashok.

The others go to my school too, but my eyes remain trained on Ashok as he avoids my gaze.

Their spiky-haired leader stands in front of the others. "Hello, Mozzy," he says.

I stiffen with fear. I don't consider myself Muslim. My family practices many religions, and I have not even decided if I am religious or not.

"Look, I don't want to fight," I say, remembering Nanaji's advice.

"That will make this a lot easier," the boy with the spiky hair says. He pushes the smallest of their group toward me, a square, stocky boy. "You take care of her."

I look over at Ashok. Would he really stand by and let them attack me?

Ashok blinks nervously. I see something familiar in his brown eyes. Fear.

The stocky boy begins to approach me. I steer my bike back, but the third boy has moved his bike behind mine.

"She's not worth it," Ashok says, his voice raised.

The boy with the spiky hair shoots him a repulsive look. "Go on," he urges, dismissing Ashok with a flick of his hand.

But just as the stocky boy shoots a fist at me, Ashok drives his bike into his back.

I use this moment to ring the bell on my cycle non-stop, hoping that some adult in one of the bungalows on either side hears.

A door opens from a bungalow nearby. "Hello, hello, what's going on?" says a woman on her porch.

The boys look at each other. There is a slight nod from the boy with the spiky hair before they scatter.

But Ashok stays put. "Are you okay?" he asks.

I am out of breath. There are so many thoughts, so many emotions swimming in my brain, but there is something I want him to know. "I may not be here by the time we get to Delhi," I say at last. "And if we do make it, I think you would be a great captain."

I can see in Ashok's eyes that my approval means something to him.

"Just remember what Coach says. The best captains have to lead by example. They have to be patient and take the time to understand their opponent."

Ashok nods. "I think I understand," he says.

I give him a nod in return. I try to calm my pulse while I quickly cycle the few meters home.

As I shut the latch-gate behind me and wheel my cycle up the garden path, I shudder with relief.

But by the following morning, we are once again thrown for a loop when we receive an email from Abbu.

My petition for your visa was rejected. My lawyer says the new government is much stricter on immigration. They say that those with political asylum who apply for visas for their families are indulging in chain migration. I told him our case is genuine and how dangerous the situation is for you and Simi. He says we can try again, but there is no guarantee, and the chances are slim under the new administration. I am heartbroken. Will call you later.

I expect Ammi to look heartbroken. But it is more than that. She looks afraid.

Suddenly, panic swamps my body. I start sobbing. Rejected. Even when I close my eyes, I can't unsee the word.

Ammi holds my hands. She phones Nani and Nanaji to say we are coming over. We need a family meeting. But I already know how this will end.

Dadu pulls out the ancient ambassador car. As we drive past the neat rows of bungalows on our lane and turn onto the main road, we pass the same trees, the same betel shop, the same bus stand, the same cake shop, newspaper vendor, and vegetable sellers, but everything looks alien. My world has gone off-kilter.

At Nani and Nanaji's, we don't waste any time.

Nani's mouth twitches. "Go to the travel agent. Pay him whatever he asks, but please leave the country."

There is so much that I don't quite understand, but I know enough to get that if Ammi and I are going to reach America and find Abbu, we'll have to do it secretly . . . like, not the legal way.

It's late. The frogs are croaking. There is a full moon out. After the decision is made, we pull out wicker chairs and shift under the mulberry tree. There is no breeze; even the rustle in the trees is caused by a restless bird. The night is still.

"Sometimes people make their own luck," says Nanaji.

CHAPTER TEN

TWO WEEKS LATER

The day has finally come.

The firecrackers and other remnants of the Brotherhood party's celebrations are gone, but the tension remains. Our days have been full with calls to the same travel agent who booked Abbu's passage to America through Mexico, hours spent talking, packing, looking for answers, solutions, and saying goodbyes.

I walk through the house by myself. The sun shines through every window and fills every room with light.

My room looks as if I will come back after school in the afternoon, like any other day. Dadi did not want me to change anything. My books are still on the shelves, the little pink stuffed elephant is still on my table, the broken blue mug with my crayons is still there on the desk, and my Beyoncé poster is still on the wall.

We've packed lightly, just a large backpack each, as Abbu has instructed.

I peep into the mirror quickly and see a smart girl in jeans and a T-shirt with her hair in a ponytail, ready for America. I wink at the statue of Ganesh as I go to the kitchen, where Nani, Nanaji, Dadi, Dadu, and Ammi are already gathered. The newspaper folded at Ammi's crossword is on the table.

Everything moves at the same time. Dadu counts the pieces of our luggage. The driver drags the bags out of the gate. Ammi locks all the doors. Dadi calls from the front gate, "Don't forget to check the French windows."

Ammi says she can't find the tickets. I pull them out of her purse. The tickets are beautiful with a red border and a photo of a maharaja. I wave them at her. We smile without speaking for several seconds. It's our shared moment of laughter and panic in the home that we must leave.

As we step from inside, I look back at my house, the kitchen garden with neat rows of tomatoes, the path bordered by forget-me-nots. I breathe in the smell of home, of family, of happier days. With each step I take away from our bungalow, I can feel my life with Dadi and Dadu in Punjab, in India disappearing.

Nanaji holds me close. "Simi, I am counting on you to take care of your ammi."

I nod. "Of course I will."

"Say namaste to America for me," Nani says with a big smile. "It will be a grand adventure."

"We really must go," the taxi driver says, glancing at his watch and cutting off Nani's words. Nani and Nanaji hug Ammi tight one by one, and Nanaji kisses the top of my head. Ammi stays still for a moment, looking at the house and the street, before stepping into the car. We are all bundled in.

Dadi and Dadu are standing at the curbside, smiling with moist eyes.

"Be careful. Don't be reckless. Take care of Ammi, Simi," Dadu says.

"I will, Dadu," I say with false confidence. But in truth it's Ammi who will take care of me.

None of us cries. We are all being strong for each other. I look at Dadi. She smiles, enfolds me in a hug, and reminds me of her favorite phrase, "Rabb tere te mehar kre, God be with you."

At the airport, we somehow find our counter, check in, and follow the other passengers to immigration. Ammi holds her handbag, slung over her shoulder very tightly with her fist clenched around the strap. Our tickets and passports and money are all in it. We know there are no people from COMBAM or the Brotherhood party here but still fear someone stopping us somehow, snatching away our chance to escape.

We reach the head of the line and my heart flutters with fear. A man with a big moustache is sitting behind the counter. Ammi hands him our passports and smiles nervously, her hands shaking. Suddenly, I feel sick to my stomach. I'm sure he will turn us away. I'm sure he knows we aren't really going to Mexico, that we have paid smugglers to take us to the US.

He peers at Ammi through the glass pane, and then his eyes linger on me. "And where are you going?" he asks.

"Mexico," Ammi says.

"And that is your final destination?"

Ammi bites her bottom lip, her answer suspended. She hates lying. I squeeze her hand hard, so tight that the blood must have stopped flowing. She stares at the officer, hesitates, and then nods. "Yes."

I exhale.

The officer compares our faces with the photographs, rubber-stamps the passports, and nods us on.

I pass from one memory to the other, of a time before COMBAM and the Brotherhood party. I remember how Ravi always came to my home the day after Eid for all the leftover kebabs. How I always go to his home for Diwali to burst the firecrackers. I remember the card parties that Ammi and Abbu went to at the Bhandaris' and Thakurs' in the lead-up to Diwali. I hold on to the image of Nanaji's library, Nanu's kebabs, the way that Dadu and Dadi sway to the gramophone. I try to make myself remember each of their scents so I don't start to forget them. However remote these memories are, they are real. One day it will be like that again.

2

Loss and Longing

CHAPTER ELEVEN

It's dark when we land in Mexico.

I stumble, blinded by the shining lights of the General Rodolfo Sánchez Taboada International Airport in Mexicali. Ammi catches my elbow and holds me up. I look at her with a smile. For a few moments I feel weightless. All the fear, anxiety, and tensions of the past weeks seep out of my body. We have landed safely.

Once we have our backpacks, we make calls to Abbu, Dadu and Dadi, and Nani and Nanaji. Many blessings and greetings later, we walk out, mother and daughter, our hands clasped. The ache of loneliness, of being in a foreign land, far away from everyone, vanishes for a moment as I pass through the automatic sliding glass doors.

The warm air that hits my skin feels so fresh after the cold airplane flight. I feel a sense of anticipation. The air smells of sand. I see a cactus on a patch of grass, its three arms sticking out into the sky. It's all so different.

I am in a foreign country, nothing like my own.

In spite of all the worries and anxiety, a thrill of excitement races through me.

Ammi and I look around the sidewalk. There should be a man to meet us, but we can't find anyone.

There is nowhere to sit. Not a bench or chair in sight. There is a parking lot, some cars, a dirt stretch, an almost-empty street across it, and nothing else. My body desperately wants to curl up and sleep.

At last, we hear footsteps approach as we wait at a designated spot outside the terminal. "Hello," a tall, tanned man in a red button-down says. "I am Carlos." He speaks in fluent English.

Carlos, we've been told, is going to be our guide. Our

smuggler who will drive us to our hotel for the night. He waves a sheet of white paper with our names on it. His face has a scar, all the way from his right eye to his chin.

I shrink back.

"Hola," says Ammi with a smile. She has been practicing some Spanish words.

Ammi can always sense when I'm nervous. She puts her arms around my shoulders. My nerves calm as I inhale her familiar smell of talcum powder and lavender soap. In a hushed voice, Ammi asks one question on the heels of another. "How will we cross? When will we cross? Will you be with us the whole way?"

Carlos puts a finger to his lips. "Not here," he says.

We follow him into a little all-night café across the road, just a few yards from the airport parking lot. Carlos orders a beer for himself, then orders tea for Ammi and a soda for me along with some chips.

"First, I have to tell you that there's been a change of plans," Carlos says.

I snuggle into Ammi, listening apprehensively. Her body tightens.

"Things are very different now from when your husband came. Things change quickly. Then, there was a short wall. It was easy to jump over. Now there is a very high wall up at the spot where your husband crossed." Carlos shows us a photo of the wall on his phone. It's made of tall iron spikes wrapped with four barbed wire rolls on both sides. "People have died trying."

Ammi stares silently. I can see the fear in her eyes.

"Now, you have two options. I could take you to the US Border port of entry in Calexico. There is a pedestrian crossing there that will take you to a US immigration station. It's called Zorilla Alley. You would make a plea for political asylum at the station. Explain how you were attacked by vigilante groups in India. Show your documents to the asylum officer. But you should know that they have been turning people away left and right."

There are so many things Carlos is talking about that I don't understand. But I grasp enough to know that this is a very unexpected change of plans.

"No one informed us of any of this," Ammi cuts in. "We want to go the same way as my husband," she says.

Carlos waves both his hands simultaneously in a double "no." "The only other way to request asylum is to do so after you have made it to United States soil illegally. But the route your husband took is far too dangerous now. So the second option is that we could smuggle you in at a different location. A spot in the desert where there is no wall, just a fence. My team of other polleros will take over. But the journey from where we can drop you off to where you will reach civilization in the US is much farther."

He stretches the map on the phone with his fingers and then zooms in on his spot in the desert. We see it in real time. It does look remote. Just an empty stretch of desert with no habitation at all. My mother looks grave.

"My men know the hills and dunes of the desert like the palms of their hands. They will guide you. They will even act as decoys if the border guards spy you. And if you are caught by a guard in the desert, they will almost certainly try and send you back." He pauses.

Ammi is clutching her purse tightly. "What would the chances be of us getting political asylum at Zorilla

Alley?" She asks the question we already know the answer to. We've already received it once before.

"It is very difficult now. They are turning away people asking for political asylum, especially families," he says, twisting his cap around. His eyes gleam in the pool of yellow light on his face that the hanging bulb above casts on all three of us.

I clutch the edge of the table tightly. We can't go back, and we can't go forward. Not without risk.

"Running through the hills and deserts?" asks Ammi, sitting a little straighter, her forehead furrows deeper with new worry-creases.

"If you make it through the desert, you are much more likely to be put in a US detention center where you can request political asylum. If you are caught closer to the Mexico side, you could be put in a camp here for months until you are sent back to India," Carlos says slowly. Every bit of me watches Ammi.

She shakes her head. My heart sinks. I want more than anything for things to be normal again, but I know that it is not safe for us there right now. Normal will take time.

The room is hot and smoky. My head hurts.

"We have to do it, Ammi," I say, unable to stay silent any longer.

"It's too risky," Ammi says softly, almost speaking to herself. She takes her glasses off, then pulls out a cloth. I know she is thinking about all our options as she wipes the lenses vigorously.

"Will it cost more?" she asks at last.

"I won't lie to you. It is more expensive," Carlos says. "But it is only a small bit extra to ensure your safe crossing."

My mother murmurs that we have already paid too much.

"In the desert, men with guns are waiting," Carlos says. Something in his eyes makes me know that he is telling the truth. "You could be robbed, kidnapped . . . They charge a toll out there, and those who don't pay the toll end up in trouble. I must pay my guides to get you through the mountainous desert terrain. It's treacherous. I am not charging any more than I must so that I can ensure you safe crossing."

I can hear the boys in the brown shorts chanting, *Mozzy, Mozzy* . . . like a drumbeat in my head.

Ammi roots in her purse and pulls out an old envelope. Money changes hands.

"I will give you half now and half when we cross," Ammi says, trying to sound in control.

Carlos nods in approval. "You have made the right decision." He counts the money, pockets it, and bangs the table with a palm.

After he's finished checking our documents, Carlos gets up and I notice that he has a gray steel revolver under his shirt. "Okay, let's go. No point in wasting time," he says.

My body freezes, eyes locked on the gun. I have never seen a gun in my life. In India no one has a gun, not even the police.

Ammi grabs my hand, lifts up our backpacks, straightens her shoulders, and leads me out. We don't speak at all as we walk from the café in the thickening darkness toward Carlos's car, outlined in the silver glint of the moonlight.

CHAPTER TWELVE

We drive for four hours in Carlos's rickety blue car. I lie down in the back seat with my head on Ammi's lap, looking up at the dark sky through the window. *It is the same sky*, I tell myself. I can see the treeless land in the distance as we speed on. The moon keeps changing the color and shape of things. The darkness is menacing.

I feel so tired. I desperately need a wash and proper food; I need to stretch my legs.

"When you are on the other side, don't tell them that your husband is in America," Carlos says. "Otherwise, they will say it is chain migration and send you back to the tents here. That's how kids get separated from their parents."

My heart beats, pounding fast and loud.

Ammi reacts even before Carlos finishes his sentence. "What are the chances that Simi and I would be separated?" Her voice comes out as a squeak.

It's hard to see outside. I look around the car as I wait for an answer. The ashtray is stuffed with Carlos's cigarette butts.

"My men are the best. They are taking you to a US crossing point where children are not separated," Carlos replies. I don't know whether to believe him, but what choice do we have?

"What is chain migration?" I ask. My voice comes out hoarse and croaky.

"It's a term some people use in the US, when one member of the family is already there and others go to join him. Like the links of a chain. Got it?" Carlos replies in a weary, deadpan voice.

I want to ask more but just shake my head silently.

I am afraid, but more than that, I am exhausted. I look forward to the room in the hotel where we will rest. A bed and clean sheets, a shower, a change of clothes, and a proper lie-down are all I want from the future right now.

We arrive at the Hotel Hacienda in a border town called Sonoyta. It's a half-built compound of cinder block and canvas tents ringed by a metal wire. Dozens of men are playing cards in candlelight under the shade of tarps hung from bamboo poles. Others are sleeping on straw mats and in outdoor bunk beds made from plywood.

My heart sinks. This looks like a camp, not a hotel. Will there be proper beds? Running water? I look at Ammi. She doesn't say anything as she pulls our backpacks from the trunk.

I breathe in the scented desert air and remind myself that we are walking in Abbu's footsteps. Carlos takes us to a counter where a man is watching TV in a small, cluttered room. They exchange a few words, and the man pulls out a key. He gestures for us to follow him. We hesitate.

Carlos points at him. "He will look after you. Don't worry. Rest, and you will be in the US in twenty-four hours." He waves as he turns around to go toward his car. We don't know anyone, and no one knows us. I suddenly don't want Carlos to leave.

"How long will we be here?" I ask Ammi.

"It's just a short transition. Chin up," Ammi says, looking at my woeful face. I smile at her use of this English phrase. I picture her at home, sitting under the Tiffany lamp, looking out at our trimmed green lawn through the open French windows, reading an Agatha Christie novel.

My heart lifts a little when we are led to a room with a toilet attached. It has a tin roof, four walls, and a window. There is furniture: two wooden cots, a rickety table against the wall, a chair and door leading to a toilet with a shower and a squat toilet. The sheets on the bed are freshly laundered. Its basic, neat, and private. There is even a fresh bar of soap.

We keep our bags on the floor. I peel off the clothes I have been wearing for two days, take a shower, and pull on a clean T-shirt. Ammi follows suit. Once we feel clean and settled, we unpack some of the food Dadi had prepared for us and eat.

I feel sleepier with each bite, savoring the taste of home.

I wake up to the sound of a rooster. For a second, I think I am on our farm in India. Ravi, Reena, and I often spent nights under the stars there. We would pitch tents, light a bonfire, sing songs, tell each other the scariest ghost stories, and finally fall asleep.

But then I see sunlight streaming through the bamboo poles in the wall. Ammi is sleeping on a wooden cot next to me. Slowly, I remember where I am.

I get up quietly so I don't disturb Ammi, and steal to the toilet. I wash up and tiptoe outside our room.

People are sleeping in a few hammocks tied to palm trees. There is a brightly painted pink stucco brick room with a thatched roof surrounded by some potted plants just past the hammocks. Plastic chairs and tables are set in rows under a tarpaulin-covered shaded area next to the room.

On the other side of the pink room is a ring of canvas tents, straw mats, and outdoor bunk beds. They are separated from the rest of the compound by what look like extremely tall humans with thick arms reaching into the sky. It isn't until I notice the thorns and flowers that I realize I'm looking at cacti.

I turn toward the dirt path leading to the reception. In the morning light it looks more friendly—a square brick room, whitewashed pale pink, with a sloping tin roof, covered with a riot of bougainvillea flowers.

I can't help it; my eyes fill with tears when I see the familiar flowers. I am far, far away from home. The sooner we reach Abbu the better. Suddenly, a large lizard wriggles across my path. I jump, but the lizard is unafraid. It stares at me, stretching its neck to look more closely. I lean down and squat on my haunches to take a closer look. It blinks, opens its mouth, and sticks out a spear of a tongue.

Delighted, I respond by sticking out my tongue too. This flat-headed creature, with its dinosaur skin and long tail, is the first friend I have made in Mexico. I watch it lope off up the dirt path.

As I step back, I almost fall over something that yelps. A large, shaggy dog. I get to my feet, worried that it might bite, but, in the end, it licks me. I feel better. I have my second friend in Mexico. "Good morning," I say to him with gratitude, crouching down to pat his head.

"Making friends?" a voice asks in perfect English. I straighten and see a boy my age with thick glasses and hair curling at the edges of his nape. He has a thin face, black hair, and bright green eyes. His shorts are faded to gray, and his dingy T-shirt has some indeterminate colored stripes.

"Just looking around," I say, scrambling to my feet. "Is the dog yours? I've always wanted one."

"As good as. Very loyal to me. He attached himself to me from the time I got off the train at Mexicali, even followed me to Sonoyta. His name is Pedro," the boy says, puffing his chest a little. He pushes his glasses up the bridge of his nose, looking at me curiously.

"I was just looking at a lizard that ran across. It's much bigger than the ones in India. And greener."

"It's an iguana," the boy corrects me. He is quite annoying, not unlike some of the smug boys I go to school with. *Went* to school with. He stretches out his hand to shake mine. "I'm José."

"I'm Simi. From India," I reply, shaking his hand. This is my first handshake. In India, we greet each other by joining our palms together, bowing our heads, and saying "Namaste."

"I'm from Honduras," José declares. "Did you hear that I survived la Bestia?"

"You were attacked by a beast?" I ask, wide-eyed but skeptical.

"No, no, it's a train. A train that's like a wild beast. It kills people. It pushed a man next to me right off the train. His hands were cut off. I sat on the roof for five days with my mother and baby sister. But we survived," he boasts.

"A train can't push people off," I say dismissively, turning to go to the reception. The boy is making up stories. Not a very reliable friend for sure.

José shoves his hands into the pockets of his shorts and stands in front of me, the dog behind him, his bones set in determined lines. His jaw is clenched, and his hands are balled into fists. I can tell how badly he wants me to believe him.

"I'm serious. It can even chop your leg off. If you grab the ladder on the back end and you fall, the wheels of the next train car are so close they'll chop you in half. I've seen it!" he states with great emphasis. "When someone falls and dies, we say, 'Se lo comió el tren,' the train ate him up," José explains.

"Why would people grab a ladder to climb onto a train? There are platforms and steps," I challenge.

José smiles in response, as if I'm missing something. "Come," he offers, pointing toward a hall made of bamboo next to the shaded area with the chairs. I follow him out of sheer curiosity past our row of five bamboo rooms. It's a largeish common room, with notice boards, toys for children, some bookcases stocked with books in Spanish, a few plastic chairs, and cushions on the straw mats that are spread out on the floor.

He walks toward the printed and hand-drawn maps of the borderlands that are posted on the notice board. José points me to a printed map of Latin America. There is a map of Mexico next to it. I squint till I find Mexicali and then look for Sonoyta. The Sonoran Desert on the map looks huge—a sea of nothing.

"Look," he says softly, his finger pointing to Honduras. "That is my country. I took a bus from here to here." His finger moves to Guatemala. I follow his finger, choosing to take his words a bit more seriously. "From here I took a bus to Mexico. Here." His finger is on a border town in Mexico. I peer at the name. It's called Tapachula.

I look for Sonoyta. It's very far from where his finger is.

"That's not where we are," I comment.

"Yes, yes, it took my family days to get here. My mother, baby sister, and I slept in a cemetery in Tapachula when we got off the bus. We had to jump onto the running train because it's a train for goods, not people. I went first with my sister strapped on my back and then pulled my mother with my hand. See how strong I am?" he says, flexing his muscles, showing off again, only this time I notice how thin he is. His ribs stick out of his chest.

I suddenly ask myself why he's trying so hard to impress me. How long has it been since he's had a friend to talk to? We are both going to a foreign country, leaving everything familiar behind. I nod and meet his eyes. I don't know him well, but I want him to know I do believe him.

I learn from José that migrants jump onto freight trains in Mexico to come to the US border. "They hang on the sides, sit on the roof for days. Many fall off and die. That is why they call the trains la Bestia—the Beast."

"Why not just take a normal train?" I ask.

"We are illegal! La Migra will catch us and send us back."

"How can human beings be illegal?"

"La Migra is the migration police. They are supposed

to send back anyone who does not have a visa for Mexico. Any of us who do not have a Mexican visa is illegal here."

"So, you don't have a visa?"

"Most people here don't," he replies flatly, matter-of-factly. He looks at me like Ravi used to when I said something stupid.

Despite the biscuits I've started picking at in the common room, my stomach lets out a loud rumble. I hadn't realized just how hungry I am.

Just then Ammi walks in looking for me. She is bathed and looks rested. Pedro gives her a lick.

"Making friends already?" she says, smiling at all of us.

I introduce her to José and Pedro.

"Have you eaten?" she asks. I shake my head.

José jumps up. "I will take you to the food."

We follow "El Leader" to the large area with chairs and tables. It looks like a mess hall. There are twenty or so people here, eating rice and beans. We walk past a man, his face so creased with wrinkles it looks like plowed earth. He is sitting with a young woman in a cotton dress, a rope of black hair down her back. Neither of them even look up as we walk by.

At the end of a row of chairs, a tiny woman with a neatly tied black bun and suntanned brown skin is feeding a baby some rice with a spoon. José walks toward her. We are just a few steps behind.

"This is my mother, Lucía," he says with a flourish and big grin, "and my little sister, María." The baby gurgles, reaching out for him as he says something to his mother in fast Spanish.

Lucía's face breaks out in a smile. She says hello in English, then gestures to the chairs opposite her. "Don't worry, I am an English teacher, so we will not need José to translate. He learned English from me."

Ammi looks relieved, perhaps knowing that she too now has someone else to talk to. She slides into the chair, leaning forward to tickle the baby.

As José and I walk to the food counter, he waves his hands in the general direction of the people scattered around the room. "Migrants from Honduras, El Salvador, and Guatemala."

He is a walking, talking encyclopedia, but I am ready to swallow all José's bits of information, as long as I get food quickly. My stomach burps as I smell the steaming rice and beans. I realize I have not been near freshly cooked food for days.

We pile four plates and walk back to our mothers. I begin to gulp down the food in front of me while José continues to tell stories. But I'm so hungry that I'm grateful for the chance to just eat and listen while he goes on and on.

"My father is in the US. We are going to meet him," José is saying.

"Mine too," I respond between bites.

"Why did you all leave?" Ammi asks.

José opens his mouth to speak, but Lucía suddenly gives the baby to José and leans toward us. This question is hers to answer.

"We are from San Pedro Sula. It's a beautiful but violent city run by gangs. I am a teacher. My husband, Bruno, was a fruit truck driver. The gangs demanded money every time he took out a delivery. It is the way things work. But once María was born, we could no longer afford to spare anything. Bruno refused to pay the gangs. One day they ambushed his truck and beat him. But that would have only been the beginning."

We listen in hushed silence. I can see a nervous tic throbbing at the base of Lucía's throat. I shiver. The early morning desert air is still cool.

"Bruno left for the US, before they could kill him. Then the gang began to come to our home. They asked José to join. Offered him a gun and a cell phone," she says, taking back the baby from José. "The whole city is poor and desperate for work. If we stayed, where would he end up? I had been saving. Bruno managed to send us some money last month. We paid the smugglers and left as soon as we could."

Ammi and I exchange a glance. Lucía's story is different to ours, but similar at the same time. We are all on edge but composed, and I begin to understand that everyone eating at this mess hall is probably feeling the same way we are. I uncurl my toes under the table, relieving some of the tension I didn't realize I'd been holding on to while Lucía spoke.

Later that day, José and I wander back toward the reception area to see if our iguana friend came back, and José boldly asks the receptionist if he has any idea of the time and date of our crossing.

The receptionist shrugs. "Maybe today, maybe tomorrow. Not long. Carlos will tell us when it is safe. He is putting a group of you together—at least four people."

José immediately speaks up. "We are five people. Simi, baby María and I, and our mothers." The receptionist and he exchange a few rapid Spanish sentences and at last the receptionist nods. "Soon, soon," he says in English.

Ammi and I use the phone at the desk to call Dadu and Dadi, Nani and Nanaji, and Abbu and tell them all the same lie. "We are fine, in a comfortable place, just waiting for an opportune moment to cross the border." We don't go into detail about the change of plans so that we won't worry them. Afterward, Ammi suggests that we head back to the room with our books. "It's been so hectic," says Ammi. "Let's just have some time to ourselves."

But just as we begin to walk back, the phone rings.

It is a message from Carlos. We are told that our pollero has arranged for us to cross the border at dawn the next day. The people who will take us across the border are called coyotes.

If a train can turn into a beast, I wonder, *what kind of beasts would we find in the desert?*

CHAPTER THIRTEEN

In my dream, there are wolves after me. I am running, running, running. A hoarse voice whispers: "Stay in the shadows, stay in the shadows." But when I turn around, they are not wolves. They are coyotes. And the shadow is too far.

It's only 4:00 a.m. when Ammi wakes me.

"It's time to go, Simi," Ammi says. I open my eyes.

It's dark and cold. I pull the sheets tight around me. "No, Simi, you can't sleep. We have to go to the border.

Wash up, put on your clothes. I have packed everything. I will wait in the mess hall for you."

I take out the book that Nanaji gave me before I left, *The Life of Mahatma Gandhi*. The leaf from my and Abbu's peepal tree is still snug between the pages where I decided to keep it. I think of Abbu as I touch its delicate veins.

I am walking in Abbu's footsteps, I tell myself again.

The man with the wrinkled face and the woman with the long braid come and sit with us at breakfast, along with José and his family. The woman introduces herself as Gina and the man as Lorenzo. She asks if she can hold the baby. Lucía hands María over, understanding the need for cuddles in this tense moment.

"We are trying to cross again," Gina says, rocking baby María. "The last time we tried, my husband was detained in the US and then deported."

The man nods and then says with some fervor, "You

must not get caught. They lock you up in cagelike, freezing-cold detention centers. My cell was standing room only."

He looks at José and I warningly. "Even children."

I feel my heart in my chest.

José, as usual, is confident that he knows everything. "I will take care of everyone. I have studied everything about the desert. I can survive anything. I survived the Beast."

Lorenzo's dark, sun-creased face looks worried as he studies our group of women and children. "I have tried to cross the desert twice now. It's hot, dry, and eats up people just like the Beast. Be very careful. Stay in the shadows. Stay together," he says, his voice hoarse and gravelly like the sand all around us.

We all nod slowly as our party breaks up. "Stay in the shadows," the man repeats as we walk to the reception to find out when we are leaving. The sound of his voice echoes, as it did in my dream.

Ammi and I phone India one last time before we slip out of the Hotel Hacienda into a wobbly beat-up van. I had stuffed my purple school backpack with my birth certificate, three days' worth of clothes, an extra pair of shoes, Nani's rosary that she had given me for luck, a handful of my favorite photos, and three books: two by Mark Twain—*The Adventures of Tom Sawyer* and *The Adventures of Huckleberry Finn*—and *The Life of Mahatma Gandhi*. But I am told to replace the books and any clothes I can spare with as many water bottles as possible.

The clothes and Mark Twain books go inside the larger backpacks we leave behind at the Hotel Hacienda to be shipped to Abbu's address in Queens. But I keep the Gandhi book with the peepal leaf tucked among its pages with me.

In the van, I take the window seat next to José to get some air. I want to see as much as possible, and I've already started to sweat from all the layers I'm told to wear—a T-shirt over my full-sleeved cotton shirt and two pairs of cotton pants, one over the other. I also tied a scarf around my waist and another around my head.

"It will protect you from the sand," I was told by the receptionist.

Our party is off to the vast Sonoran Desert. José, Lucía, baby María, Lorenzo the wrinkle-faced man, and Lorenzo's long-haired wife, Gina, are with Ammi and me. The oldest is close to sixty and the youngest is six months old.

The road is dead quiet. We pass shuttered garages and food stands. I recognize the large yellow and white cup-shaped flowers of the cotton plant. Soon they will grow as tall as me and the white cotton fiber will tumble out of the black spotted boll.

The ground cover changes shape and color as we drive. As we get closer to the desert, I begin to see other kinds of cacti. Plants become tangled, cacti get larger, the number of trees multiplies. Some have branches almost as high as the banyan trees at home. They stand like tall watchtowers along the empty desert road.

"That's the saguaro. It can grow fifty feet and be two hundred years old," says José from under his cap. This is the twelfth fact he's recited in the past fifteen minutes. I leave this one alone with no follow-up questions.

"That's a real coyote," José says, pointing at an earthbound animal before we drive too far away. It's a grayish-brown creature, about two feet tall with large, pointed ears and a bushy tail tipped black. "They keep to themselves but can stalk humans. They are invisible and silent in the desert, but they move fast," continues El Leader.

The landscape seems to go on forever. Shrubs sprout from dry cracks in the sand, their spiky stems and bright yellow and red blossoms sway in the breeze like some kind of weird desert animal. As usual, José enlightens. "Oh, the trees with the yellow flowers are paloverde, and the bushes are called creosote."

José points to an animal browsing sparse grass to the right of us. "Antelope," he says.

Suddenly, the car begins to slow. Now we can all feel how hot and dry it really is.

"I'm going to drop you off along the highway near the border," the driver says, "but you must get out fast." He passes us some watermelon to eat as we get close to our final stop.

The trees and fields are gone. The dust and gravel road lead us to an endless sandy stretch speckled with short, stubby trees. No grass in sight. Just earth, stones, sand, and the sky.

There are wooden stakes about five feet apart running along a dirt path. We are told that less than forty yards separate the road from the border. If I squint, I think I can see the barbed wire fence that we are meant to crawl under. But an ocean of desert on the other side of that fence separates us from civilization in the US.

"Border," says our driver, a short, stocky man with a square face, as he stops the car. He points to the mountains. "A scout from the mountains will guide your coyote's way. They have radios. They have binoculars. They can see border guards from mountains. They will talk to your coyotes from there."

There are sand dunes and knife-edged mountains slicing skyward from the desert floor.

He explains what we should do after we reach civilization in the US. "Don't walk far. Just look for a road. Go there and wait. A Border Patrol car will find you.

Don't wander. Stay together. The desert is a devil."

His fright infects us. Our bus is silent. I can see Gina, head down, praying. Lucía kisses a pendant. Ammi and I shoulder our backpacks without saying a word to each other. We hold each other's hands tightly as we quickly step out of the van.

There is not a moment to waste. The driver has already started reversing. We notice a movement near the paloverde tree. A hand beckoning. The coyote who will guide us through the desert is waiting, his brown shirt and pants blending into the background. He looks only a few years older than me.

I hold Ammi's hand tight.

Stay in the shadows.

Then, a second coyote emerges from behind a saguaro cactus. He appears much older and sturdier than the young one in brown. This one is dressed in well-worn camouflage pants. He looks at our group, assessing our ability to cross the desert. His eyes stay a little longer on me. But there is a confidence about him that puts me at ease.

"Mateo," he says with a hand on his chest. "Santiago," he says, pointing to the younger one. Mateo hoists a backpack filled with water, food, and medical supplies on his back. He is not interested in our names. He puts a finger on his lips to motion our silence and hands us each a big floppy hat, extra wide-brimmed to cast a shadow over our faces, necks, and shoulders. "Sombrero," whispers José, as we adjust them on our heads.

I put a finger to my lips. "Quiet," I say.

It is still dark as we begin our journey on foot, slipping through a gap in the stakes. Cacti spines slice my arms and ankles as I crawl through the hedges and brush. No time to wipe the blood. I'm told this is the easy part.

I keep my eye on Santiago, the young coyote in front of me. Ammi is behind me, then José, Lucía with baby María wrapped in a blanket with only her eyes visible. Gina and Lorenzo trail behind them with Mateo at the very end. We walk in a line. We don't talk for fear of being sent back. But every now and then I risk a glance at Mateo, who looks as though he might as well have a map of the desert embedded in his coarse palms.

We walk like that for three hours, not making a sound. The sun rises and grows hot. The sand is so soft that my feet sink into it. Every once in a while, the ground tries to steal one of my shoes, but Ammi makes sure I put them back on and ties my shoelaces tightly. She has not done this since I was in kindergarten. I smile weakly, so spent in the dry heat that I can barely talk. She pats my cheek as we begin again.

Everything around us looks empty and lifeless.

All of a sudden, Mateo at the back shouts something, and Santiago in front stops. Our entire line comes to a halt in the blazing sun. We are on a dirt road beneath the south side of a tooth-shaped mountain. Mateo says something in a deep, commanding voice, then points toward the mountain and says, "Kino Peak." They continue to speak to each other in Spanish.

I look at José.

"Mateo is leaving," José says. "He says another coyote

is waiting for us on the far side of the valley ahead and we must stay on the south side of the peak to meet him at the other end," José translates. My heart sinks.

I have so much sand in my throat that speaking hurts. The blinding heat has left no extra energy in my body, but I try to argue. I sneak a glance at Santiago and wonder again how old he is. Fourteen? Fifteen? I can see the fear in his eyes. "He can't do that," I say. "We paid Carlos for two men to be with us all the way."

José translates but Mateo shrugs. Ammi steps in.

"These trails are almost invisible. We have a baby with us. What if there is an emergency? How well does this boy know the desert? Please tell Mateo not to go," she implores.

José does his best to convince our two desert guides, but Mateo's impassive face doesn't change expression at all. Santiago stays still, awaiting his orders. Mateo, who has been carrying our supplies for us this whole time, suddenly dumps the entire lot of provisions—two gallons of water, medical supplies, some beans, and a sleeve of saltine crackers—on the sand.

I am already too thirsty and tired to continue. We look at the pile in despair.

"Please," Ammi tries. "We will pay double when we reach the end of the desert."

But Mateo has already turned to leave, as if it was his plan all along.

I am surprised to see that Ammi does not even argue, and understand then that she doesn't have the energy. I look at her. She puts her arms around my shoulders.

Silently, Santiago begins to strap our supplies to his back. Sand is beginning to stick to his faint moustache. I wonder if he even knows how to keep in touch with the scouts in the mountains around us. The ones who are supposed to guide us on their walkie-talkies.

We drink some of the precious water, to make our load lighter, and eat a saltine cracker each. My lips are chapped. My upper lip has cracked. Along with the cracker, I can taste blood.

Stay in the shadows.

I look at Ammi. Her head is covered but her dupatta scarf is matted with dust. She notices my chapped lips and quickly splashes some water on one end of her scarf and wipes my face. The cold sensation is the closest I have come to relief.

Santiago tells us to hurry. The sun is rising higher and soon the desert will become a furnace. Everyone picks up a few of the supplies. José's weather-beaten face is so dried out from the sun that it is hard to tell if he is worried, but he has found the energy to translate for the group. The rugged mountains and the bone-dry valley stare at us as we begin.

But almost immediately, Gina and Lorenzo declare that they are going to walk ahead on their own. They say they can walk faster without us children and they know the desert just as well as this young boy who is supposed to be our guide. They take one gallon of water from us.

Now we are six.

CHAPTER FOURTEEN

We are two families. Two mothers. Ammi with me, Lucía with María and José. The sun is blistering so bright it looks white. José's mother takes off the jacket that covers her blue cotton frock. Ammi's dupatta is tied over her head. Even our sombrero hats feel heavy.

Baby María looks exhausted. Ammi sprinkles some water into her mouth while Lucía holds her up. She shivers, and my mother touches her forehead.

"It's burning," Ammi says. "We must hydrate her."

Lucía looks anxious. "Sunstroke," says my mother. "Don't worry, I am a nurse."

Gently, José holds baby María in his arms while Lucía mops her forehead with a wet cloth. We continue walking.

I am so tired that my feet drag, without any feeling. I shift my weight from one leg to the other. This road that we are supposed to be looking for is feeling farther and farther away. I am not even sure if Santiago knows the right path.

My skull aches.

"Why is it taking so long?" I ask José.

"Santiago is saying it's because of our group. That it's always slower with women and children."

I manage a scoff. Santiago is beginning to remind me of Ashok and the other boys who didn't think I had it in me to be captain. What I would give to be back in India right now. Back on the field with my stick.

José and I keep quiet. We decide to tie a rope around the big plastic container that has our water and drag it in the sand. It bumps on the ground and raises a tiny cloud of dust with each step. At least we don't have to carry it.

Just a little while longer, a few minutes more, and we will see the road where the border guard patrols, I keep telling myself. I swallow my saliva, but there is none. I look down at my feet. I can feel my blisters and wish I could take my shoes off. Ammi knows what I am thinking. She shakes her head in a silent "no." A helicopter flies over us like an evil vulture looking for prey.

I trip and almost fall, but Ammi's hand stops me. None of us looks back. We don't want to slow down. There is no way we can go faster, but we don't want to go slower. José, El Leader, is silent for a change. He pulls out some peanuts from his pocket and gives them to me. Even in this parched moment, he shares. I chew every nut into a paste before swallowing so it can last as long as possible.

On the far horizon, the sky is blue, with no border road, just dunes. I am tugging the plastic container without looking back, just putting one leg in front of the other as we walk uphill. In an instant, the rope breaks and our jug rolls down.

We watch in horror as the cap comes off and water flows out. José runs after it.

Our water supply. Gone.

My body falls to the sand and tears stream from my eyes. I am shocked there is any liquid in me at all. I don't look at José or Ammi, just at the ground, my legs stretched ahead of me. I am sure we are walking to nowhere. I have never been so thirsty or parched. It's like a deep, spreading craving in every part of my body.

For several moments, I don't notice anyone. Then I feel Ammi hug me.

Lucía and José are sitting next to me.

Baby María has fallen asleep again and is not waking. The only water we have is in the bottles in our backpacks. Ammi pulls one out for me and I notice José does the same for his sister. I take a few sips and sprinkle my bottle on María's body. She revives. But I know we still have a few hours to go. Maybe more. Our supply won't be enough.

Santiago, who has been standing over us as we mourn our dwindling supply of water, leads us to the shadow of a sand dune and tells us to wait while he goes to look for a nearby creek. We are so completely dehydrated that we just let him go.

But after what feels like an hour, he still hasn't returned.

It's then that we begin to understand. Our young guide has deserted us.

I am too tired and defeated to react.

We are five now—two women and three children. Ammi says we must begin walking again with the mountain on our right. "That's the only thing we know. And the safest. The sooner we get to the road, the better," she says, looking worriedly at Lucía and the baby.

But just a few steps later, Lucía slides to the ground. Luckily, José is able to grab baby María. We have no idea what to do. José looks close to tears now. Ammi splashes some water on Lucía's face. I notice it's the last of Ammi's bottle. Lucía opens her eyes but does not get up. She sits without moving.

"She hasn't drank nearly enough. She's given all her water to the baby," comments Ammi. Her voice is raspy, hoarse from the sand and the dryness.

I look around. The path has vanished. At last, I say what everyone is thinking. "We're lost."

There is no reply.

The sky is a solid mass, stretching forever. There is not a single cloud.

José slides to the ground next to his mother. He unties his laces and takes off his shoes. The blood dries in no time. He points to a cluster of scorched trees and brush. It looks near but in this shimmering haze it's hard to judge. "There might be some shade there. María will faint if we keep sitting in the sun like this."

"We have to do something," Ammi says. She takes a look at us tired children, sighs, and gets up. "Wait here. I will go to the cluster of trees to see if there are any edible leaves that the baby and Lucía can chew on and, if a miracle occurs, some water for you two. They told us that good Samaritans leave water near trees for people like us, remember?"

The blood rushes to my head. I imagine Ammi walking away and disappearing, just like Santiago. But I know that she will always come back to me. She will take care of everything. I cling to her and she hugs me tight. The pain rises from my belly to my throat.

"Let's just wait here for the second coyote," I say, pleading. "Don't go."

She strokes my hair. "I am going for you. If I don't get water or something for you to chew on, you will pass out just like Lucía and the baby."

I look at María. The gurgling baby is barely able to keep her eyes open.

"Let me come with you."

"You have to conserve your energy."

I know Ammi. Once she has made up her mind, nothing will change it. I do as she asks. Slowly, my hands slip off from around her. Everything inside me is empty. She wipes my brow with her sleeve, kisses my forehead, and hugs me hard. Then she leaves without looking back.

I keep my eyes peeled toward the black trees. I can see Ammi's silhouette in the distance against a blur of sky and sand. I am no longer sure if it is her or a tree. Lucía is fading again. José fans his mother and the baby with his shirt. It's just four of us.

I can't see Ammi anymore. The desert has swallowed her. The crown of my head is itching, but I don't have the strength to lift my arm. There is no movement in the direction of the trees. Where is she? How can so much change in forty-eight hours?

I shut my eyes and hope when I open them, I will be home and not in the set of this dystopian movie. Abbu will be cooking, Ammi arranging flowers, Dadi playing the gramophone, and Dadu's TV clashing with her music. I imagine the sound of Dadi's prayer bell as she waters the tulsi plants, the sound of her fingers snapping three times before plucking a few leaves to prepare the plant for pain. I wish then that she had done the same for me. I open my eyes but there is only the endless sand and the hazy trees, blackened and twisted, like bent knuckles.

My heart is burning. All this time I've been telling myself that I am following Abbu's footsteps, that this will all be worth it once we are together and safe. But now I can't even see Ammi's footprints in the sand. Every trace of both of them has disappeared.

José springs up with a determined air. Both Lucía and baby María are barely breathing.

"We can't wait any longer. We have to take Mama and María to the trees. Maybe Santiago or the second coyote will show up there," José says.

My heart closes in. One of us must stay in the spot where my mother left us.

"I will stay here and wait for Ammi," I say. I'm not sure I have the strength to walk even if I wanted to. José is still the fittest of us all. After all, he did survive the Beast. He will go to the trees and come back with news of Ammi. Maybe she is too tired to walk back.

I can see the trees from where I am, so we can't get lost.

"We will come back for you," he says.

I nod, terrified.

I create a little tent for my head by tying a scarf to the top of my backpack. I spread a shirt under its narrow shade and place my head under it. I am alone now.

Hours pass, maybe minutes. I don't know the difference. I can see neither Ammi nor José. I lose all sense of time. The sun is relentless. Even if it's not true, I feel I am the last person on earth.

⸎

I can hear Ammi calling me. My gums hurt. I can't reply. Her voice fades and I can't hear her anymore. Now my ears hurt. Is my brain on fire or is it my lungs? Still, I keep my eyes open, turned toward the trees, waiting for Ammi.

Instead, I see a man walking toward me. He looks like a white spirit in the haze. Finally. It must be the coyote we are expecting. Or perhaps an angel from the heavens or one of those good Samaritan water carriers, which is the same thing. He says something in Spanish, but there is no José to translate. He gives me a can of sweetened water. I drink greedily and splash my face, my head, my arms, my toes.

My brain begins to function again. I exhale. Then I drink some more water. I wet my shirt and scarf and wipe my face, arms, neck, and toes.

"Muchas gracias," I say, using the few words I had learned at Sonoyta. He nods gruffly.

After a few minutes he asks me to follow him. "Vámonos, vámonos," he says.

"No, no." I try to resist. "I am waiting for my mama."

The man nods patiently but does nothing. He probably thinks I am delirious. I don't have the strength to argue in the scorching heat. I just sit down and refuse to move. This is the spot she has left me, and this is where I will wait.

I try to explain and know just to repeat the word *Mama, Mama, Mama* a few times. I point to the trees. "Mama there."

"Ah!" he grunts. "Yes, yes. Mama. I take you to Mama," he finally says. And I wonder whether Santiago told us the truth after all. He could be the second coyote who was supposed to turn up. "Santiago?" I ask.

"Sí, sí," he replies.

At that I make a snap decision. I get up and follow him. He leads me just behind the sand dune where we have spent the last long horrible hours. Lo and behold!

There's a dried-up creek bed with tangles of mesquite and paloverde. It was so near; how could we have missed it?

I remember Lorenzo's story from Hotel Hacienda. He had tried to cross the desert twice and both times ended up going round in circles, until he was picked up by the Mexican police. He said he kept missing the trail. "I was marking directions by the sun. But the sun moves in the sky and all the dunes look the same."

We begin to trawl the banks, and scattered in the underbrush, we find water cans, torn shirts, and food cans left behind by other migrants. This is the trail Santiago was talking about. For a moment, I think I see Ammi's dupatta fluttering. But it's only a mirage. The sun is going down now. But where is Ammi? Where are Lucía, José, and baby María?

My footsteps are heavy, my hands are swollen, my thoughts are muddled. We are hiking toward a giant cactus. I can't see the black trees anymore and I begin to wonder if the coyote is really taking me to Ammi. But I know that I can't leave him. He has water and he knows the routes.

At last, we reach a patch of shrubs and cacti. My heart lifts as I see people walking toward its shade. I know it must be my mother, José, Lucía, and baby María. That the coyote did not lie. I thank the sun, the moon, and the stars, and even the sand and the sky. "Thank you for finding my ammi. Thank you, thank you," I murmur to the universe.

But as we come closer, I see it's two men with three children. One of them is José. Where is Ammi? Where are Lucía and baby María? I look around him and into the distance, but I can't see our mothers anywhere. The other two are a boy and a girl I don't know—a little older than us. Both are dressed in rugged blue jeans and T-shirts. Their skin is covered with sand, the soles of their shoes are coming off. I am sure I look like them. I certainly feel like them.

One of the men has a red scarf tied around his neck, and as we get closer I notice that the other has a scar running down his right cheek. He is dressed in a black hat, a black polo shirt, and black jeans, as if the heat doesn't faze him in the slightest. On his feet, he wears Reeboks with unexpectedly pink soles.

The man with the scar pulls out a pack of cigarettes. Each of the men take one, light it, and then herd us children together. Scarface jabs José in the arm, pushes him toward me, and says jovially, "Your friend is alive. You are lucky."

José smiles half-heartedly.

My new guide hands me some crackers and a can of water. He ushers me toward José and the other children before he lopes off to talk with his friends. We sit down as the three coyotes huddle a little farther away.

I wet my handkerchief, wipe my face, and remove the sand from my eyes. The two other children in our group do the same. But José looks uneasy as he glances back at the men smoking their cigarettes nearby. We smile shyly at each other.

"I'm Simi," I say to the other two kids.

The girl points to her brother and says, "Oscar," and then toward herself. "Elena." We nod with a few weak hellos. The two siblings lie down in the shade with wet hankies on their eyes, their backpacks under their heads. They are simply too tired to talk.

But once the men are safely a little distance away, their backs turned toward us, José springs upright. "Simi, listen to me. These people have tricked us into walking away from our mothers. We have to be careful. They speak very good English."

"What do you mean, tricked us?" I ask urgently. "Where are our mothers? Where is Ammi?"

"We had just found Ammi when these men found us," José said. "We thought they had come to help us. Your mother had twisted her ankle. That's why she hadn't come back. She had found the leaves for the baby though."

I process the fact that Ammi is alive. At least that is something, I think to myself. "So why are they not here with us?" I ask, puzzled.

"These men, the one with the scar on his face, told us that you were dead."

CHAPTER FIFTEEN

It takes all my energy to keep myself from bursting into tears.

"Your mother fainted when they told us you were dead," José continues. "They asked me to go with them to fetch your body and your things. And they were so impatient that Mamá told me to be quick while she looked after your ammi."

A tear drops from my eye onto the sand. José breathes in, looks to see they are not watching us, and squeezes my hand, which rests on the sand between us. "The good news is your ammi is alive. And you are alive. But now we have to get away from these men."

"Why would they tell her I was dead?" I say, wiping my tears.

He looks down as he mumbles, "They are collecting children they find lost in the desert to sell them."

"How would you know that? Sell us for what?" I ask, hoping this is one of those stories José comes up with to prove he knows everything.

"I heard these two talking while we were walking here. They plan to sell us into labor. They were saying that the boys will be good for the egg farm . . ."

"What about me?" I whisper hoarsely, my heart thumping.

He squeezes my hands. I can see he is very afraid. He talks with his head down, so that the men cannot see his lips move. Elena and Oscar listen without saying a word. But it is clear from their eyes that they understand.

My heart sinks. There is a whirring in my ears. My hands clench into fists.

"They can't do that. My ammi and abbu will find me,"

I say fiercely. I want to cry but am so dehydrated that there is no water in my body for tears. We look at each other, wide-eyed and terrified. José draws question marks in the sand that he quickly erases when we hear someone approach.

Scarface is back, a coke in his hand. "You can call me El Lobo," he says, taking a sip. "I am your coyote. I will get you to safety. Don't worry, I have helped more than fifty thousand children get into the US."

All of us children look at each other. We are too scared to say anything. We can't just run away into the desert. We don't know this vast unmarked terrain, and El Lobo has all the water.

I can hear Nanaji's voice in my head. *The* way *we fight for something can be just as important as what we are fighting for.*

"El Lobo, can you tell us where our mothers are?" I ask. "Perhaps we can go to them first?"

"Your mothers are with ICE," he says.

I try to understand. "Ice? In the desert?"

He looks at me as if I am stupid. "ICE is the US

Immigration and Customs Enforcement agency. Your mothers are with them. Remember those helicopters? Those choppers belong to the border guards. Your mothers are in safe hands by now."

His lie filters through my foggy brain while I try to think of what we should do next. Did I hear helicopters? I can't remember. I push my hair back and sit up straight, trying to determine whether there is a shred of humanity in El Lobo's eyes.

"Come with me and I will take you to them. You don't want to die in the desert, do you?" asks El Lobo, his thin moustache wriggling, his left eyebrow raised. None of us responds.

For now, we don't have a choice. We must walk on.

El Lobo walks at the front of our pack. He is the only one leading us now. The other two men have gone, and I wonder if there are more children out there that they intend to round up. El Lobo keeps stepping away for frequent cell phone calls.

José is silent. I take some slow swigs of water. Oscar and Elena trudge forward, but every now and then they look back at us. Clearly, they trust José and me to decide what to do.

For a moment, I wish that I had brought my hockey stick, if only to remind myself that I am still a captain. A leader. I can still carve out a path for others to follow. But how is anyone supposed to find the right path when there is only a sea of desert on all sides?

For now, at least El Lobo knows the way and has given us enough food and water to revive us for the time being. But I can see in José's eyes that he is looking for the right moment to run.

Suddenly, a loud hum rings in my ears and I wonder if my body is beginning to fail me once again. But I know that sound. It's not in my head.

It's the sound of a car engine. It gets louder as the seconds tick by.

In the distance, I see a white pickup truck with a green stripe from the corner of my eye. It has a US flag on it.

I remember then how my father had managed to enter the US by surrendering to them. Immediately, I know that I would rather take my chances any day with the US

Border Patrol over this man. I make the decision once more to walk in Abbu's footsteps.

I am weak and dehydrated, too tired to do much, but I somehow manage to untie my scarf from my backpack and wave it in the air.

José sees what I'm doing and chimes in. "Help! Help!" he yells.

Elena and Oscar do the same, waving the clothing they've been using as shade.

El Lobo lowers his phone. "Stop!" he seethes in a whisper. "That's Border Patrol!"

But a man from the car shouts back through a megaphone. "Who's there? Stay where you are!"

I look at José, and I know we're thinking the same thing.

"HELP! HELP!" we shout with every breath we have left in us. Elena and Oscar cry for help as well.

A plume of dust rises as the car turns and picks up speed in our direction.

With a look of sheer panic, El Lobo scuttles off into a bed of shrubs, leaving us behind.

I feel my legs give way as I sink to the ground, my energy spent.

Someone splashes water on my face and I open my eyes. It is a blond-haired, white-skinned woman in a green khaki uniform. I slowly look around me. There is still not a cloud in the sky, but the sun's rays are gentler, less harsh.

The woman in uniform gives me a bottle of sweet-tasting water. Somebody pats me down and then lifts me into the back of a white van.

"I'm here," José says. "Try to breathe. Drink."

Elena and Oscar are here too.

I take a few sips before the panic sets in again. "Ammi?" But no one understands. They just shake their heads.

The uniformed woman pulls out a pen and paper. "We are Border Patrol officers," she says, before asking us a string of questions. "Name?" she asks loudly.

I answer. "Simi Singh."

She continues with the other children. Father's name? Mother's name? Address in the US? Relatives in the US? Age? Nationality? Country of origin? I lose track of her questions. I can't even remember how I answer each question that is thrown at me.

"Where am I?" I ask, dazed, surrounded by these uniformed people asking nonstop questions. The van is baking. It's suffocating to be parked in the desert with so many people in this tin vehicle.

"We're seven miles away from the official US port of entry in Arizona," the woman says. "We'll be taking you all to a processing center in Ajo."

"Where is my mother?"

"We have no idea. You must have walked nearly thirty miles," says the officer. "For now, you will remain in our custody." She hands us each some kind of crackers and bottled water and then jumps into the front seat next to the driver. I will myself to breathe and tell myself to stay calm. We've escaped El Lobo. We have food and water. For now, that is enough to sustain us.

In the back of the van, José and I exchange glances. What should we tell them about our families? Is it better to tell them I am alone, or to tell them I crossed the desert with my mother? Do I give them the phone number of my father? Or will he get in trouble?

José and I clasp hands as the van rattles over the earth. "We have fathers in the US. They will help us find our mothers," whispers José to alleviate some of our worry.

We drive for miles down the desert road with nothing but sand and shrubs on both sides. Nothing has felt better than the air-conditioning in the van and cold sweet water on my tongue. But I would crawl back to the desert if it meant being reunited with Ammi.

Think of something positive. For now, I am safe. I am strong enough to take care of myself until I can find Ammi. *Sheekh kebab!*

I wet my scarf and wipe my face, arms, and neck. I take out my hairbrush and brush and tie my hair in a ponytail. As I wipe away the sand from my neck and face, I begin to feel human again.

The sun has begun to set. The desert hills cast long shadows. The land fades from brown to purple and finally to black. The van zips by a rattlesnake that is sunning on the rocks and slows for a hardy cow that wanders freely across the road. Finally, we pass the first building I've seen in what feels like years—a small tire repair shop and a fueling station.

The road becomes broader. We are on the main road of a town. I can see AJO written on a big blue sign. We pass a church, some shuttered shops. Ruben's Barber Shop, Dairy Queen, an office building with a beautiful mural with the sign AJO COPPER NEWS. A café. I wonder what keeps this small community busy in this little town, in this lonely stretch of hot desert.

And then a white glow shines over a compound that sits by itself in the desert. We are driving toward it. The big plot of land looks like a prison, ringed by a yellow brick wall, guarded by scrubby mountains. Cars, vans, and buses crowd under a green aluminum roof.

We slow down near the entrance.

AJO BORDER PATROL STATION, US CUSTOMS AND BORDER PROTECTION FACILITY.

I see the US flag, with another blue flag just beneath it, flying from a flagpole.

Abbu, I think. *I made it.*

But where is Ammi?

CHAPTER SIXTEEN

We line up and do exactly as we're told. There is a group of children just like us being unloaded from another van. We shuffle across the shadowy dust, making our way into a shed like a flock of sheep.

Inside, men, women, and children look as if they too have just crossed the desert. They sit on concrete benches. Their clothes are covered in dust, their faces caked with sand, their postures drooping.

Ammi must be here, I tell myself.

Officers in green khaki uniforms sit behind computers on gray desks piled high with files and papers. In front of us, a man in a brown T-shirt and blue jeans is being patted down. An officer wearing blue plastic gloves turns out the man's pockets, looks inside the hems of his jeans and belt, and then asks the man to take off his shoes and turn them inside out too.

"It's to check for drugs," José whispers.

I look up at the giant clock in front of us. Ten p.m. It feels like a lifetime since we left Sonoyta at four this morning. It's not even been twenty-four hours, but my world has changed. I have changed. I have survived the desert, but I have lost Ammi.

What is the point of any of this without her?

José and I wait on a cold, hard cement bench. Elena and Oscar have been ushered to a different side of the shed in a different line. Ten or fifteen people wait in line before us. It's close to midnight by the time it is José's and my turn. We are patted down. An officer pulls out our pockets and makes us open our shoes. A woman takes my backpack and empties out just about everything in it—my extra shoes, clothing, my silver belts, even my hair bands, my book, and Nani's rosary that she had given me for luck.

She leafs through my photos—the one with Abbu and Ammi where I am in a hockey uniform holding a hockey stick, the one where I'm dancing with Dadi, the one where Dadu and I are in front of our farm tractor, and the one in my pink dress with Nani and Nanaji at the lake. She flips through the pages of my book and finds the leaf. My heart plunges as she picks it up to throw it away. But then her eyes meet mine, and an understanding seems to pass between us before she gives me a small smile and gently puts it back in its place.

I want to cry but I'm able to hold a straight face. I have to stay strong.

I have to find Ammi.

And then together we'll find a way to get to Abbu.

"I think my mother is also here. Can you check? Please," I ask the lady as she digs into my backpack.

She looks at me with something like sympathy, nods, and tells me to wait as she walks over to the man at the desk. Finally, she beckons me.

José and I both hold our breath.

"You came with two other children, not related to you. No adult," the man at the desk says.

"I was separated from my mother in the desert by coyotes. Maybe another van brought her here?" I respond. "She thinks I'm dead."

The agent at the desk softens.

"Let's look. What's her name?" the lady officer says.

"Henna Ali," I say.

The man looks down the list and looks at me with pity in his eyes. "There is no Henna Ali here."

"Could you try Henna Singh?" I plead.

He scans the computer again. The other people in the line behind me are getting restless.

"Sorry," he says, shaking his head. "We need to move the line along."

My heart sinks. What if she's still out there? What if the coyotes took her?

In the meantime, the lady throws all my things into my backpack and then into a bigger plastic bag, knots it, and tags it with my name. "You will get it when you leave. Don't worry," she says, flinging it onto the racks behind her. She gives me the tag.

I want to howl. But there is no point. It won't bring Ammi back. Last week seems so far away, like the life of some other girl. I can hear cries and wailing all around me as we walk farther into the facility.

"It's the screening room," the all-knowing José tells me. But I am so glad we are still together.

We get our fingerprints stamped and our photographs taken. Officers sit on swivel chairs behind computer screens. I am so tired, I could drop right to the floor. I go through the motions, as requested, too exhausted to ask questions.

Name.

Age.

Country of origin.

Relative or sponsor in the US.

They ask me if anyone brought me here. Was I tricked, duped, coerced? They check my birth certificate and passport. They hand me a piece of paper called a Notice to Appear in immigration court. I'm listed as an unaccompanied minor—a UAC. But what does this notice mean?

"When can I talk to my father?" I ask. But this agent doesn't appear to be as kind.

The agent doesn't answer, just shouts, "Next in line!"

The next desk man gives me a piece of aluminum. I turn it over.

"What is this for?" I ask, bewildered.

"It's a blanket," the agent says.

I am too stunned to reply. How is this hard, tin thing supposed to be a blanket?

"May I take a shower?" I ask the next agent I see.

"Maybe tomorrow. After twelve hours," he says, pointing us farther inside.

We are marched down a long corridor. Some of the walls have quotations by John F. Kennedy, Abraham Lincoln, and James Madison, and photographs of border guards on horses, driving ATVs, bending down and helping children. I try to picture one of Gandhi's quotes here. *"The greatness of humanity is not in being human, but in being humane."*

Just then, as I'm ushered in one direction, José is pushed in another. I freeze.

"Separate cells for boys and girls," the man tells us.

"Hold on to this aluminum," José says, a last bit of parting advice as he waves goodbye. "You will need it."

My eyes fill with tears.

I am absolutely on my own now.

The first thing that hits me as I walk into the holding area is the stench of urine, dirty clothing, sweat, and toilet water.

The second thing I feel is the cold. I now understand what José meant when he called it a hielera—a freezer. I had longed for coolness in the desert and now the universe has punished me with an icebox.

I can't decide whether what I'm seeing is true. There are ten cages made of chain-link fences with rows of human beings wrapped in aluminum.

Even the animals in the zoo were better off. At least they could see the sky, the sun, and the moon. Here, there are no windows.

I want to cover my eyes, ears, nose, but I do the

opposite. There is a glaring white light shining down on me, even though it is past midnight. Children lie with adults in tight rows. The Border Patrol folks work at stations and desks in a kind of glassed-in area. They can look out through the glass onto the floor and into our cells.

It feels like a jail. Like I lost my mother and I am being punished for it. As I walk to my cage, I look around carefully, my eyes wide open, my ears on high alert for a familiar voice, to spot Ammi.

We reach my allocated cell. It looks crowded. There are thirty or so girls and young women, packed in this room with only one toilet.

I find a spot near a wall, as far from the toilet as possible, put the aluminum blanket on the floor, sit on it with my back to the wall, and try to regroup.

Through the glass, I look into the eyes of the agents behind their desks. Why are they allowed to be there while we have to stay here? None of it is fair. But I can see the sympathy in some of their eyes. Like the woman agent who let me keep my leaf. It is the only positive thing I can think of to hold on to as my eyes fall shut.

CHAPTER SEVENTEEN

It must be morning because somebody brings us oatmeal and ham sandwiches to eat. The sandwich is as ice-cold as the concrete floor.

I don't feel like I slept at all. I feel just as exhausted as I was in the desert. The white light is too bright. There is always at least one child crying. I haven't wanted to drink water so I don't have to use the bathroom in front of so many others. I still have the same sick feeling inside me that I've had since Ammi left to look for those leaves for Baby María. As if I have eaten something rotten.

I repeat my father's phone number over and over again inside my head so that I won't forget it if someone asks. I wonder if he's driving his taxi right now. If he's waiting for a call from us. What are Dadi, Dadu, Nani, and Nanaji thinking now that it's been so long since they've heard from us?

I scold myself. I have to stay clearheaded. I have to think of something positive. "Chocolate ice cream," I say to myself, savoring the taste as if I am biting into it.

The agents look almost as exhausted as we do. They've been walking around, counting all of us children every hour throughout the night. Some of them have had to take mats away from children to give to younger or sick children.

One of them comes into our cage and settles down in a corner, smiling at us after breakfast is passed out. He's tall and thin, with short brown hair. He looks at us with kindness. "If anyone would like to play a game, please join me," he says in Spanish and then in English.

I notice then that he's brought a stack of board games in with him.

My heart jumps at the opportunity to ask him questions. Surely, I can ask about a few things while I play with him.

I get to my feet, head down, and begin to walk slowly toward him without looking at anyone. I don't want anyone to reach him before I do, but most of the others are too tired to move.

I work up the energy to put a smile on my face by the time I sit in front of his stack of board games.

"Hello?" I say timidly.

His eyes are kind. He smells clean. Like soap. His manner is polite, friendly, and official.

"Hello," he says, holding out his hand to shake mine. "I am Pablo. What would you like to play?" He waves his hands over the boxes of games at his feet.

"I'm Simi," I say, returning his handshake and pointing to the Scrabble board. It's one of my favorite games. The officer raises an eyebrow. I don't think he's used to speaking with children who can speak very good

English, let alone play a game with English words.

I sit cross-legged opposite him. We spread out the board, pick our tiles, and begin to take turns. I toy with words, saving some letters for later. I change *slander* to *islander.*

"You're an expert," he says, winking.

"My mother taught me," I reply. Saying her name makes my heart hurt. She loves reading. "Very good at crosswords."

"She taught you well," he says with a smile, studying his tiles for a word. That's my opening.

"We crossed the desert together, but some coyotes separated us and now I can't find her. She wasn't in the computers yesterday." My stomach is churning. "Do you think some other Border Patrol could have picked her up?"

He looks up, a sad look in his eyes as I wait for his answer. Something tells me that this is not the first time he's had someone ask him this question, and that the answer is not always a good one. "I'm not so sure. If she is not in the computer system, it means she isn't here."

My breath catches in my throat. I try to speak without my voice wobbling.

"I am sure she will show up in the system sooner or later. Maybe in another facility. You're not to worry," he says in a gentle voice.

What a ridiculous thing to say. How can I not worry?

It's my turn. I want to use this time to talk and not think of big words, so I make *host* into *ghost*. I can see that he wears a wedding ring on his finger. I wonder if he's ever had men come to his door to make sure there is no beef in his fridge.

"Do you have children?" I ask.

Pablo smiles. "Yes, two. One is a boy your age. Little taller than you but not fond of word games at all. Just baseball and hockey," he responds with a laugh.

"My father was a hockey champ. He's a taxi driver in New York now." I brush a wisp of hair behind my ear and look at him pleadingly. "Could you help me phone him?"

"There is a procedure to all of this. And so many people here that we have to take care of," he says. "But I will try. I promise."

I shoot him a look but say nothing. He cocks an

eyebrow. Then when I nod in understanding, he smiles. It feels good to be talking to someone.

"Your father must be worried sick. No child—no parent for that matter—should have to go through this. The system needs to be fixed," he adds, shaking his head.

I can see he is tired and frustrated, so I don't pester him anymore. Soon our game is over, and he gets up to leave.

He extends his hand for me to shake once more. "Duty calls. It's been a pleasure, Miss Simi," he says as I watch him go.

I exhale a long breath and wonder how I will distract myself until I can make a call to Abbu.

Pablo does not come back that day. Nor am I called to make a phone call. I feel depressed and cold. The frozen burrito they give me for dinner stinks. I throw it away and eat the two cookies and drink one of the juice packets that the pantry lady had given me.

I look at the clock once more and estimate that I've now been here a little over twenty-four hours. I remember what Abbu said, that he was here for three days. How will I make it that long? Each minute that passes is a minute that Ammi thinks I'm dead.

A girl near me clears her throat. She is about eleven. Brown-haired and brown-eyed. She waves at me and then pats the floor next to her. Another younger girl is sitting with her.

My heart warms with the gesture. I make my way over and sit next to them.

We smile. The older girl passes me a cup of water. I've been holding back tears for so long, but now the gates blow open. So little can mean so much when you are alone.

I don't know how long I cry. It could be a minute or an hour. But the two girls stay with me until the tears begin to slow.

Finally, the older one points at her own chest. "Sonia," she says. She points to the girl that looks like her younger sister. "Valería. We are from El Salvador." It's hard to say much since I can't speak Spanish, but they can speak enough English for us to understand one another.

"I'm Simi. From India."

She turns over my hand, looking at my palms. "Beautiful!"

I had forgotten about the flower motifs hennaed on my palms that have just barely begun to fade. It's only been three days since I left India. Dadi and I had gotten it done by a popular henna artist just outside the gurdwara, the day before I left. My eyes moisten again as I think of home, Dadi and Dadu, and Nani and Nanaji. It feels as though the patchwork of our family has been ripped at the seams and thrown to different corners of the world.

"Don't cry," Valería says, reaching out to wipe my cheek with her tiny hand.

They smell just like me. Sweaty and stale.

"No shower?" I ask, making hand gestures to show water from above. Valería giggles.

"They came around twice to ask, but it was night and we were asleep each time."

"How long have you been here?" I ask.

"Sixteen," says Sonia glumly, pulling her little sister close to her.

My heart plummets. "Sixteen days?!"

There is no way I can find Ammi if I am caged like this for sixteen days. I envy Sonia and Valería. At least they have each other.

The sadness that overwhelmed me a moment ago is replaced by something else—an impulse to push through it.

I think of José. I've only known him for two days, but he's the closest thing I have here to family. If there's anything I know about him, it's that he knows how to get information. And if José has learned anything about where his mother is, that will lead me that much closer to Ammi.

CHAPTER EIGHTEEN

Another eighteen hours pass. I have been here for nearly two days when a lice infestation breaks out among the girls in our cage. All the children are scratching madly. Somehow, it hasn't made its way to me. But when I notice that the girls who come down with lice are taken to the infirmary, I get an idea. To get to the infirmary, you have to pass the boys' cell . . .

It may be my only chance to talk to José.

That night, I pretend to get itchy. I scratch and scratch

behind my ears, just like the stray cats who live in our garden at home. It's not long before a woman in a blue uniform leads me past a converted loading area, where dozens of boys are huddled. It is the middle of the night, so they are asleep beneath their aluminum blankets.

I try to walk as slowly as possible as I peer through the fencing, searching for José, but the woman in the blue uniform ushers me along.

"You are contagious," she says.

I pray that I will get another chance on the walk back.

At the infirmary, she cleans my face and puts on some ointment. Even though I'm not actually infected, it makes me feel better. Everything looks dilapidated and moldy in the infirmary, but it has a window. For the first time in thirty-six hours, I finally see natural light. It nearly burned my skin off in the desert, but after so long without sunlight, I'm ready to forgive it.

A plump, black-haired woman in a gray smock does a full medical check-up. She doesn't find lice, but my skin is red where I have been scratching myself, and the woman determines that it must be an allergy. She gives me some ointment. Then she gives me a smock to change into and takes me to a bed with clean sheets. Despite her no-nonsense air, she seems caring.

"Shouldn't I go back to my cell now?" I ask, hoping to pass José's cell again.

"We need to make sure you are not contagious first," she says. "You'll sleep here tonight. Tomorrow, someone will escort you back if the itching stops."

She has begun to remind me of Dadi. "Will you take me?" I ask.

The woman sighs. "I'm not sure I'll be here tomorrow. We are volunteers. Coast Guard officers. Just helping out."

She's about to leave when I decide to take my shot. "I am not an unaccompanied minor," I say in one breath. "My mother was with me. She was separated from me in the desert by some bad men. She might be here, if the coyotes haven't taken her away," I tell her.

Her head falls and she turns around and sits at the edge of my bed. "Have you heard of the Zero Tolerance policy?"

I think I have, but I can't recall. "Vaguely, but I am not sure what it means." I wish I had paid more attention to the conversation at the Hotel Hacienda.

"It means that the US government will have zero tolerance for parents migrating with their children to the US."

My brow furrows. This means nothing to me.

She continues: "Children who cross the border into the US will be separated from their parents and kept in different places. Eventually, both will be sent back to their country," she explains. "It is supposed to be a deterrent," she adds offhandedly.

"What is a deterrent?" I ask.

I can feel the heat of her eyes on me. She sighs. "It's to keep foreigners out of America."

I think she is trying to warn me not to tell the officers that I have come with Ammi. I meet her eyes. I can see how upset she is, how mad this rule makes her just as it makes me.

As politely as I can, I say, "I don't care if Ammi and I are sent back to India. All I want to know is that she is alive. I just need someone to help me look her up."

She glances at me hard, then nods and gets up. "Give me her name, and I will try my best to find out about your mother."

She does not know Gandhiji's wisdom that Nanaji once shared with me. Gandhiji had said an unjust law is itself a species of violence and that it should be resisted by nonviolent gentle acts. But she is standing up for right and justice in her own small way.

Perhaps she has heard of Gandhiji afterall.

But the next morning, the plump, black-haired woman is not there. A different guard walks me back to the infirmary. I cross the converted loading area where fifty-some boys are rubbing their eyes and waking. I slow down, scanning the faces.

One of the boys waves. "Simi, Simi," I hear.

It's José.

My heart skips. He runs over to the edge of his cage

and I can smell his stench instantly. I realize I must smell the same. We smell like the animals in a zoo.

"Please, can I talk to my friend?" I beg the guard. He nods and allows us a few minutes. I am so, so happy. "Have you found anything out about where your mother is?" I ask José.

José shakes his head. "Not yet, but I won't give up until I do. And when I do, I will have news of yours."

My stomach drops. We are grappling with the stuff of nightmares.

"There are some men and women in a warehouse a little farther up," he continues. "They could be there. I saw some of the bigger vehicles being moved out and some men and women being taken in. Maybe the computers in those warehouses are different," he adds wistfully.

The volunteer is beginning to get antsy. But José does not fail to give me new information as I get ready to go. "If we don't find them here, we will find a phone and track down our fathers. We're all being sent to a shelter very, very soon. All of us children who were picked up three days ago."

Our time is up. I don't know how to feel when the guard ushers me back to my cell. What if Ammi is here? What if I am being taken farther and farther away from her?

My two friends from El Salvador welcome me back with big grins.

We eat our ice-cold burritos together. "Did you find anything out?" Sonia asks. "How long do we have to stay in these perreras?"

"Not long," I say. I tell them what José told me—that all of us children are going to be moved to a shelter very soon. She recites a few Hail Marys. Her little sister imitates her very cutely. "What's a perrera? I thought we were in hieleras?" I ask curiously.

"A perrera is a dog kennel. We are in dog kennels in hieleras," she says, waving her hands around her. "Freezing dog kennels," she adds with emphasis. My heart aches as I follow her gaze. The bodies sleeping around me in the shining overhead light, inside different cages. I don't answer Sonia as the ache gets deeper and darker. But then little Valería comes and cuddles me. "Tell me an Indian story."

We lie down next to each other, the aluminum foil sheets covering us as I begin to tell her a story about the lion who drank up the pond. I try to tell it just like Ammi used to tell it to me.

When I wake up on my fourth morning here, there is already commotion in our cage. Our breakfast is here and we are being rushed to finish.

"Your friend José was right," says Sonia, who is already up and about. "We're leaving. All the children are being taken to some place today."

I feel like a puppet whose strings are held by an unknown puppet master.

As we line up to leave, Pablo appears in our cell and walks over to me. He tells me I am going to a shelter in a town called Phoenix. *What kind of shelter? How is this going to get me any closer to Ammi and Abbu?* I want to ask, but his tone is rushed. "I just wanted to say goodbye," he adds. "And to let you know what is going on, so you feel less disoriented. It's not far, just a few hours. They have everything designed for children. You will be better off. The shelter is run by Health and Human Services."

"How will we go? Will all the children be together? What about my father? Why don't you send me to him?" I manage to ask. There are tears in my eyes. It feels as though I am being taken farther away from Ammi. And I don't want to be separated from José. And what if the volunteer from the infirmary is able to look up Ammi somehow? How will she find me?

Pablo looks a little sad at my questions. "It's not in my hands. The Office of Refugee Resettlement decides." He looks at my woebegone face as he straightens. "You are going to a place that has proper showers."

I smile at that.

He leans down to my level. "I know there are too

many names and departments and agencies for a little girl to understand. But you are smart. You can remember words so easily. You will get the hang of it."

I smile forlornly.

"Come give me a high five," he says, raising his palm toward me. I clap my palm on it. He smiles. "See? You have learned an American greeting already."

I hope I find someone as kind as him in the shelter. One kind person can make any experience more bearable.

"Good luck," he says, waving goodbye.

I wave back, walking into the same warehouse through which we had come only a few days ago. There is a man in charge of the bags. I give him my tag and I get my prized backpack back in return. My precious leaf is with me again. I take out my photo with Ammi and Abbu and look at it before walking to the van outside.

As soon as I step into the van, José's smiling face is there to greet me.

A wave of relief floods over me as I go to sit next to him.

"Mama is alive, here in the US," José says in a whisper. "Baby María is with her. They have been taken to some place called a detention center, but she was here in Ajo too. She was in the hospital so they had not put her in the central computer."

My heart is racing. I hug him tight, stink or no stink.

"José, is Ammi with her?" My voices shakes with excitement and something else. Fear. I don't want his answer to be no. Or worse . . .

He shakes his head slowly. "I don't know, Simi. I was allowed only thirty seconds with my mamá. In the middle of the night, a guard came to take me to my mother. They asked me if I recognized her. Then they asked me what her name was. How I was related to her. Once they were satisfied, they took me back. They said they were sending her and María to an ICE detention center."

My head hurts, my stomach clenches. I still haven't been able to call Abbu. I don't know where my mother is. But she must be with Lucía. She must be.

Tears wet my eyes. I look out of the window, chewing

my bottom lip. I can feel José's eyes on me. When I turn back, I see that tears are threatening his eyes as well.

"I don't understand why they won't take me to her," José says. He looks both devastated and confused.

"It doesn't make sense," I say in agreement, my voice a little shrill. "You are just twelve years old. Do you know where your mother was taken? I am sure Ammi will be in the same place."

José shrugs. "I don't know yet, but we are all in some central database and we will be connected soon. And as soon as we are, we will find your mother too. I promise."

He holds out his hand and I take it in mine.

We are both alone. But we are in this together.

3

Rescue and Reunion

CHAPTER NINETEEN

After hours of driving, our bus finally pulls up to a compound surrounded by brick walls, iron bars, and barbed wire. The name of the shelter is displayed in the reception area. Casa Phoenix. Behind the entrance is a playground. Beyond that is a row of green-walled rooms with small, curtainless windows that look like clusters of eyes spying on us. My heart sinks. It feels like yet another prison, only this time with a playground.

"*Casa* means 'home,'" whispers José.

But it looks nothing like home.

During our journey here, some of the children talked about how they expect us to be at the shelter for months. I feel like I've forgotten how to breathe. I can't be away from my family for that long. Even if I have to walk back through the desert to Mexico.

Our escort hurries us off the bus. "They have bed space for you all now," he says. "But we have to do your intake first thing. Otherwise they may take other children."

I feel yet another wave of frustration. *What is an intake? Why can't I just go to New York where my father is? Why am I not even allowed to call him?*

José and I hold each other's hand tight, our backpacks slung behind us. So far, we have managed to stay together.

The first thing they do is take away our backpacks in exchange for some clothes and a piece of paper with a number on it. We are walked out into a hallway lined with posters on how to braid our hair, tie our shoelaces, brush our teeth. I feel some relief. At least this might mean we'll get toothpaste and toothbrushes.

We walk farther and farther—inside a brick building, inside a chain-link fence, inside a wall of iron bars. The farther we walk, the more imprisoned I feel.

How will anyone be able to find me here?

The next thing I know, I'm being "processed" yet again in a place called the Intake Room.

"My name is Paul. I am your case manager in charge of conducting your initial intake interview," says a plump, blond-haired man sitting behind a computer on a desk. His face is red and full of acne marks. "I will gather your family information. If you don't have a family member in the US, I will find a possible sponsor for you."

My breath quickens. Somehow this feels like the most important moment of my life. This man named Paul can decide my fate, and yet he looks like he's about to fall asleep.

"I do have a family member here. My father is a taxi driver in New York," I say as politely as I can.

Paul's face is stony. I wonder if he hasn't heard me or doesn't understand my Indian accent, so I repeat myself. "My father is here in the US."

His eyes are fixed on his computer. I swivel my chair a little to see what he is reading and see the queen of hearts and a club of spades on his screen. A *card* game. His eyes meet mine when he notices what I'm doing and he glares at me. I've already made him into an enemy.

There are dark circles under Paul's eyes. His skin is flushed. His shirt crumpled. The blinds are down over the window behind him. His desk is messy and cluttered. There is an overflowing ashtray near the window. The plant in the corner is wilting. Nobody has watered it in days. If they can't even look after a plant, how will they look after us children?

He proceeds to ask me questions that I've answered dozens of times before in the past three days. Name, age, medical history, country of origin, parents, sponsor details. I sound out the answers as loudly as I can to make sure he understands me through my accent. My backpack is returned to me just long enough for me to hand over my documents. I pull out my birth certificate, vaccination card, school certificates, photos with my family, and passport. He barely glances at them before throwing them into a folder and dumping them in a plastic box. All my documents are out of my hands.

He eyes me with dislike. "We have to establish your age," he says.

"My birth certificate is in the folder you just put in that plastic box," I reply.

But he continues to eye me suspiciously.

"I'm tall for my age," I argue.

Still, he continues to look at me like he doesn't believe me. "You will have to go through age determination. They will use radiographs and dental X-rays," he says at full volume. "They will check the development of your third molar tooth to determine your age." He speaks with a lazy voice, as if he's giving me directions to the bathroom.

Suddenly, I miss Pablo. I miss the Coast Guard volunteer who sat with me in the infirmary. My heart trembles and everything starts to happen so fast. What are these tests that will tell them how old I am? What if they stick me in an adult facility? Where is José?

Paul drones on about my fate through a wide yawn. He takes a sip of coffee and recites from a piece of paper without even looking at me. My ears begin to ring as he goes on and on, saying words and phrases I don't understand. Age verification. Attorneys. Interviews with family members. Case files. My cheeks are hot with worry. I try to imagine Nani and Nanaji, Dadu and Dadi stirring their tea around our kitchen table, but I know that they must be aging by the hour, worried sick with every minute that I'm unable to contact them. And then I catch something of interest.

"You will be able to talk to your father once a week. If we can prove he is your father, then you will be reunited with him," Paul says, and then stops to take a breath.

I jump into the pause.

"When can I call him? Can you find my mother in your database? She is lost in the desert; the coyotes may have left her there. They tried to separate us," I say.

Paul nods, impatiently. "Yes, yes," he says.

"You're not even writing anything down," I say with a hint of anger.

His turquoise eyes stare angrily out of his round face. I have annoyed him again.

"Please look for my mother," I ask, gently this time. "She thinks I'm dead." It feels like all my strength has been drained and everything I have left rests on this request.

"I am sure they're searching." He puts out his hands in a gesture that seems to say, *There's nothing any of us can do now.*

They. Who are *they*?

He is not even trying. He hasn't even written down her name.

Heat rises to my head and before I realize it, I'm standing up.

I'm walking across the room to the white door. And then I begin to run. If no one will help me find Ammi, then the only person I can rely on is myself. I run out through the doorway and down the flight of concrete steps. At the last step, someone catches me by a belt loop on my jeans.

"Let me go. I need to find her!" I say, trying to escape from the grip.

"We can't let you go. Not yet," says a woman's voice.

I sob, repeating Ammi's name repeatedly. *Henna Ali, Henna Ali, Henna Ali.* I beg the woman holding me to let me find my ammi. "No one else will. Please. I want my ammi," I wail.

I look back at the woman and see that her face is kind. This only makes me cry harder.

I hear nothing, because it is impossible to hear anything when your whole world is gone. *Gone.*

"We will help, but we have to check you in first," she says as she helps me get up and walk up the stairs. Slowly, my legs begin to straighten, even though everything inside me is empty.

"I am your counselor. My name is Sophia," the woman says. She wears a knee-length skirt, a boxy shirt, and flat brown shoes. But her tight bun is a contrast to her kind eyes. She puts a hand on my forehead. "I think you are sick," she says.

Now that I think about it, I do feel hot. I didn't think

to ask myself if it was normal, because nothing feels normal anymore.

Sophia hands me a cup of water and some toast. "You're burning up. Come with me. We'll finish up your intake later."

I'm in a room with windows, where at last sunshine can pour in. Someone gives me clothes to change into. I slide in between cool, clean sheets. I take the pills they give me and dream of Ammi.

She is sitting by my bed, stroking my hair, telling me a story. It's about the day I had cleared out her desk drawer and found some dried mustard flowers at the back.

Don't you remember where they're from? Ammi says. *They were from when you, Abbu, and I had gone for a walk through the mustard field, remember? The mustard was golden yellow and knee-high and there were sparrows and bees lodged in the stalks. The wind rustled over the stalks, and the smell of mustard, half spice, half perfume, filled our nostrils. You said you wanted to hear the bees and the birds laughing and talking.*

It was very bright, and I wanted to take you into the shade, away from the sun. I was worried you would get sunstroke. So, I tried to bribe you. I said I would give you the doll's tea set that Nani had given me when I was your age. I had stored it in my cupboard. All the little cups and saucers, the teapot, and the sugar bowl were wrapped in separate pieces of tissue paper and kept in an old chocolate box.

You had always liked it. You used to unwrap it and we would lay it out on the dining table and sit and admire it in the sunlight. It was pale-pink porcelain and it looked very fragile and delicate.

As you got up, you plucked some mustard flowers and said you would make tea from them to serve me in the tea set. You forgot to make the tea, but I kept the flowers to remember the day when you talked with the birds and the bees.

"I remember that day," I tell Ammi before my eyelids become heavy.

I am drowsy.

"Good night, Ammi," I say, content at last.

CHAPTER TWENTY

The pillowcase under me is wet with sweat when I wake up. I hear a collection of strange sounds—a thud, the clomping of feet, doors closing. I am in a white room, with white windowpanes and white furniture. Even the people talking to one another are in white clothes.

I don't want to get up. If I hide completely under the covers, maybe Ammi will come back like she did in my dream. I slide under the sheets and shut my eyes tight.

There are people standing by my bed, talking.

"She's been sleeping on and off for sixteen hours, but her breathing is even."

Somebody puts a cool hand on my forehead.

I keep my eyes shut, pretending to be asleep.

"Her fever is broken at least."

I recognize one of the voices as the woman from yesterday. Sophia.

"We will release her after a medical exam when she wakes up," another voice says.

"Good. She still has to complete her check-in," Sophia says. "Can somebody take her to Paul after the medical exam? Tell her it's necessary to enter the data to find her parents."

My ears perk up when I hear them mention my parents.

"Yes, we'll tell her—"

"Good morning," I say, sitting up in bed. The three adults turn around.

A lady with a stethoscope dangling around her neck comes over. Sophia and the nurse are just a few steps behind.

"Glad to see you are okay," Sophia says. "I will take you to Paul when you are done. He still needs a few things from you."

Two medical aides take my height, weight, and blood pressure and ask about vaccines. Ammi would have checked in greater detail. They tell me that I will be taken for an age verification test next week. And that the sooner that test happens, the sooner I'll be able to call Abbu.

"But if you let me call Abbu, he could tell you that I am twelve," I argue.

"I understand that it's frustrating," Sophia says. "But this is how the system works. It's part of the procedure." She escorts me back to Paul. My shoes creak as I walk down the hall.

"Please explain where we are to her and what her next steps will be," Sophia says to Paul. Her eyes are stern. "Be patient. She is scared and disoriented."

Paul looks up from his desk and whines out a "Yes, ma'am." At least he listens to her.

I remind myself to be brave. Now that my fever is broken and I've gotten some rest, I'm determined to learn everything I can. Like Nanaji always says, *Knowledge is power.* I breathe in deep. The more I learn about this *system*, even if it doesn't make any sense, the more prepared I'll be to find Ammi. It's not so different from studying another team's game tactics in order to figure out the best way to get through their defense.

Paul eyes me speculatively, one eye almost closed, after Sophia leaves. "Do you know where you are?"

"Not really," I answer.

He lets out a long sigh. "You are in Casa Phoenix. It's a shelter contracted by ORR for more than four hundred children like you."

Four hundred children! All separated from our parents. It can't be, but it is.

"What's ORR, sir?" I ask timidly, even though I know he doesn't have much patience.

"Office of Refugee Resettlement. A US government department." His tone is as bored as it was yesterday.

"How long will I be here? My father is in the country. In New York. I can go to him and free up space for you here," I say. It's worth a shot. "It will save you the work."

"First we have to verify your age," Paul says flatly. "That may take a couple of weeks."

I feel my cheeks get hot. A couple of *weeks* feels like a lifetime. A couple of weeks is fourteen days that Ammi thinks that I'm dead. That Abbu and my grandparents will spend worrying the same thing. I look at the light streaming in through the crack they have left open in the window. "May I speak to my father on the phone at least?"

"Until your age is verified, you cannot speak to your sponsor."

My heart plummets. "He is not my sponsor, sir. He is my father."

He holds up his hand to stop me from interrupting. "Let me finish."

I hold my tongue, though I have a million questions. The sooner I contact Abbu the better. But before I'm able to ask, he begins reading his script again.

"Before placing you with a vetted sponsor, the ORR will do background checks, fingerprinting of the sponsor, and in some cases, a home visit. We often request documents, like birth certificates, to verify relationships. Our staff arranges calls . . ."

He reads this script so quickly, I can barely understand it.

"Excuse me," I interrupt. "May I take notes?" I ask.

He sighs and passes me a paper and pen.

I try to concentrate as his eyes fall back to his paper and he begins to speak again.

"While here, boys' dorms will be separated from girls'—"

"But my friend is here. He's a boy. José—"

"Like I said: Boys' dorms will be separated from girls'."

Does that mean I won't be able to see José at *all*? But Paul is already speaking again before I can cut in to ask more questions.

"If a sponsor does not pass our screening or cannot produce appropriate documents or stops communicating with our staff, we investigate deeper. Once the sponsor"—I open my mouth, but he stops me—"your father is verified, I will make a discharge plan and coordinate your travel arrangements, maybe even escort you to your new home city."

He has finished.

"How can Abbu reach me?" I ask.

He raises his eyes to look at me. "He will get an A-Number."

I wince. Does Paul only speak in government language?

I plod on. "What's an A-Number?"

"It's an alien Number, a number where you can be tracked through the system. Your father will have the code to know where you are anytime. So it's easy for parents to find their children," he replies impatiently.

The System seems far from easy.

"But how will my mother or Abbu know to ask for an A-Number? Who will they ask?"

I can see Paul is restless now. "Next!" he yells, dismissing me. But when he presses a button on his table to let the next person in, I nearly squeal.

José walks through the door.

I am beyond grateful that we will have the same case worker, even though he may be the worst.

"Make sure to ask him about the A-Number," I whisper to José as we pass each other.

José gives me a wink.

I am escorted away with a cluster of girls, down a hallway painted with colorful animal murals. We turn right down another hallway with a long line of maybe nine or ten rooms.

I am taken inside a room with six bunk beds. There are two other girls in the top bunks eyeing me curiously. The walls are decorated with sketches and printouts, including a typed quote: *When you are sad, just think that to God, you are special.*

Our room has a window and air-conditioning. Sunlight pours onto the desk in the corner and I'm relieved to see that there are trees outside our window. Tall grass like the zacate that José has pointed out runs beyond the perimeter. There are light switches, so at least we will be able to sleep in the blessed darkness of the night.

"Simi!" I hear the harmony of two familiar voices.

I turn around, delighted. Sonia and Valería light up as we rush to hug each other tightly. They point to the bed allocated to me. My backpack is already there. I will have Ammi's and Abbu's photos, the Gandhi book, and my precious peepal leaf.

I sit down on the bed, exhausted after the long morning. I am about to lie down when a staff member walks into the room, scans us all with her eyes, and then walks away.

"Every fifteen minutes someone comes and checks on us. You will get used to it," one of the girls in the top bunks says. She is black-haired with pale, freckled skin.

Sonia introduces me. The girl with the freckles is Ana. Thirteen years old from Guatemala.

The other girl peeks over the bed. "I'm Anita. From Brazil. Fifteen." She wears a red bead necklace with matching red earrings that dangle against her neck. She notices me looking at it. "I made it during our craft class. I can teach you."

At least my roommates are friendly. My eyes travel to the instructions pasted to the walls.

"Those are rules," little Valería explains. It seems that there are rules for every minute of the day. "The staff makes banging noises until we wake up," says Valería earnestly. "Then we make our beds."

I grin. She is so cute. She comes over and sits by me, putting her arms around my waist, leaning her head into me. "Will you tell me a story tonight, Simi?"

I start a story Abbu used to tell me.

"Once upon a time, a princess was locked in a tower surrounded by a garden and a moat. The evil king, her captor, wanted to marry her. But she did not want to marry him. But he had one weak spot. He loved betting. So the princess decided to outwit him with a bet. She said, 'I bet I can solve any puzzle you give me.'

"The king, intrigued, gave her a small box with a maze and a silver ball inside it. The challenge was to push the ball out of the maze and out of the small hole at the end of the box.

"She moved the ball to the left and it rolled into the center. She moved the ball right and it hit a wall. Perplexed, the princess got increasingly annoyed. She almost broke the puzzle by stomping on it.

"Frustrated, she went off into the garden and saw a butterfly on a rose. It sat on a petal for a mere second and moved to another flower, exploring the whole garden. Her mind quieted down as she looked at the entire garden with its pathways, trees, shrubs, and many colored flowers. She went back to the puzzle. This time she decided to look at the whole maze, rather than just the ball. In a minute she found a path for the ball to roll out of the maze . . ."

If I had not been so tired and if my bed had not been so deliciously comfortable, I would have told the part where Abbu explains the moral of the story. *Look at the big picture, always*. But I fall asleep.

Suddenly, there is a knock on the door. Another staff member walks in. "Go and sit on your own bed!" she yells at Valería. A moment later she is calling someone over the radio, asking the person at the other end to translate to the kids in the room that they are not allowed to hug. Not even if they are sisters like Valería and Sonia.

Valería's head falls and my heart hurts all over again.

"How can they not allow you to hug your own sister?" I say. "How is any of this fair?"

"Those are the rules," Anita tells me as soon as the staff member leaves. "If you do something bad, they report you, and you have to stay longer."

Longer. It's only been four days since I lost Ammi. Five days since we packed our things into the van at the Hotel Hacienda. Two weeks ago, I was celebrating the Punjabi New Year with Ravi and Reena. I was sitting at the kitchen table with Nanaji and Nani, Dadu and Dadi. What I would give to see them right now! Two weeks is a lifetime. In two weeks, everything can change. I've seen it happen before. I suck in a breath, summoning all my strength.

This time, I tell myself, it will change for the better.

CHAPTER TWENTY-ONE

There is a loud bang. I am up and staggering on my feet before I even remember where I am. I look around for another rock that surely must have been thrown through the window. I look for Ammi and Abbu.

"It's only the staff banging outside to make sure we wake up," says Sonia, who is already up.

I gather myself. "What time is it?"

"Six a.m.," she answers.

Everyone is moving about mechanically. Sonia shows

me how to make my bed. We take turns to use the shower and the toilet: Little Valería is first, and I, as the newest bunkmate, am last. By the time I finish, it's time to line up for breakfast.

Eating is a rushed affair. We grab what we can. All four hundred of us have to eat before our required classes. We line up from the smallest to largest, take our portions, sit down, and eat. It's scrambled eggs, a piece of toast, and orange juice. I see the others take milk and muesli as well. We gobble it all down quickly so that the next batch of children can come and eat.

I look around for José, but I can't see him. *He is nearby,* I remind myself.

After breakfast we have exercise in the open yard.

"Arms forward. Fingers to toes. Don't bend knees," says the trainer. You can hear knees crack and breaths huff. Seventy bottoms are up in the air. "Count to ten." My body is still tired and sore from the desert heat. A bird sings from a tree outside our compound. Its whistle is sweeter than the notes of a flute. It reminds me of home.

We are shepherded to classes with other girls and boys,

and I immediately look around for José. But I can't find his familiar face among the sea of other children. There is one teacher for thirty-five children. The first class is mathematics. She begins to write *X*'s, *Y*'s, and plus, minus, and multiplication signs on the blackboard. I learn "good morning," "good afternoon," and "good night" in Spanish. Another teacher comes to teach us English. I am way ahead of the other students. My English is much more advanced than theirs and my mind wanders.

Every minute is a minute not spent trying to get Abbu on the phone. If I could only speak to him, I could tell him where to find José's mother. I could tell him to ask her what happened to Ammi. There has been so much information spat at me, but the information I have to share is answered with silence.

I force my thoughts away from the negative. Outside, a tall palm tree sways—gentle and powerful at the same time.

"Are you with us?" the teacher says. He notices that I am not listening and asks me to read from a book by John Steinbeck. But when I read, he starts laughing. "Is that singing or reading?" I try to tell him that my singsong tone is normal in India. That the tone or pronunciation do not matter as long as we can communicate with one another. He calls another student to read. I sit down with a red face and look back to the palm tree outside for comfort. I tell myself that a breeze will come soon and calm me. I ask to use the bathroom to cry, but if one child needs to use the toilet, then a staff member has to find five others who also want to go.

I sit and wait.

Finally, it is time for recreation. One hour and fifteen minutes of free time. We are given permission at last to use the common room—play games, read, chat, go outside and play. But I am too exhausted to do much. I find a spot of shade under the palm tree, breathing in slowly. Being alone can also be a luxury.

The days have structure. Daily life and services are strictly regulated, with rule after rule piled on.

Do not touch. Do not run. Do not share food. Do not use nicknames. Do not sit on the floor. Do not misbehave. Also, it is best not to cry. Doing so might hurt your case. There is a line for everything. Even to go to class, eat, or go to the bathroom in the daytime. Our escorts won't take fewer than five girls anywhere.

On my second day, Ana has a fit when she is told to wait for the bathroom. They give her an injection of something to calm her down. They seem to inject any child who shows the smallest sign of emotion, anger, or rebellion.

The mornings drag on until lunchtime. We are mostly served rice, beans, chicken, and some vegetables, the occasional pizza or burritos on a good day. I love the burritos. They are the closest to Indian roti. But how I miss our ordinary daal and curried vegetables. I promise myself to never fuss over Ammi's cooking again, just as long as she's returned to me. The meat is stringy and has a faint smell as if it has gone bad. I long for Nani's kebabs. Even the pile of boiled, peeled potatoes are tasteless. Still, they are fresher than the meat. I put forkfuls of the rice into my mouth and swallow the dry potatoes whole. I drink two glasses of water to wash it down.

Except for Ana, all the girls in my room are soft-spoken. They have grown up working on farms, helping their mothers plant and harvest crops. They seldom question an adult, even when they are tired and annoyed. They are not as impatient as me. I think they admire the fact that I speak up, challenge the staff and teachers, even if the elders look bored or irritable, which is what Paul is like most of the time.

Perhaps this is why they elect me task leader of our dorm. Each dorm's task leader is in charge of supervising daily chores—room sweeps, laundry, bathroom cleaning. I try to make it fun whenever I can. We horse around with the buckets and brooms, mops, sponges, Pine-Sol, and bleach. But if we older girls try to do the chores of the younger girls, who can barely hold the brooms, we are reprimanded. Rules are rules.

Cameras scan our classroom, the hallways, even the dining and recreation areas.

Service request forms are required for everything—even if we need sanitary pads.

After a full week, I find it harder to take in the deep breaths that I've been using to keep myself calm. I picture Abbu, frantic. What if he's trying to contact me here too? What if he has no idea where I am?

I ask Paul at our weekly meeting, "Any chance I could use your phone?"

"No," he says flatly.

"When can I talk to my abbu?"

"Who?" he asks.

"My father. You know, my sponsor." I speak slowly, in words that he relates to, so that he can understand me.

His answer is that of a robot: "You will be allowed one weekly ten-minute call, supervised by staff."

"It's been a week," I respond.

His face flushes redder. His eyes bulge. I am challenging him. He looks as if he will burst but then pulls up something on his computer. "Next Saturday," he tells me.

"Why can't I talk sooner? You said I am allowed one call a week."

I am met with a gruff reply. "We have to get your age determination test results first. This is the policy of the Office of Refugee Resettlement."

I try to stop myself from grinding my teeth. "Have you heard any news of my mother?"

"She's not in any database," he says indifferently.

My heart breaks, but I try to stop it from shattering completely. "She was on the bus with José's mother, Lucía. If Lucía is in the system, she can give you more information."

But I am dismissed before I'm offered an answer.

That afternoon, Anita teaches me to make intricate bracelets. There is a huge supply of colorful yarn, always available, even after craft class, in the common room. I make six to give as gifts when I meet my family and four as keepsakes for my friends in the shelter, to remember me by when we leave. I make an especially beautiful one for José, for when I finally see him.

On my second Sunday here, we are given a motivational speech about patience, having faith in God, and how to use the time in the shelter to prepare for what comes after.

I recede into my thoughts and think about *before.*

Before the rock crashed through our living room window and our lives changed forever. Before the pamphlets started littering our doorstep and men came looking for beef in our fridge. Before Abbu was attacked. Before Ammi and I set off into the desert.

It is hard to imagine an after.

It's all taking so long.

When I get back to my dorm, I write another letter to Abbu and Ammi to tell them how much I miss them. I write these notes on pages hidden in my math worksheets so as not to violate yet another rule: No writing in the dorm room. No mail is one more rule. I keep the letters safe in a folder for the day when Abbu, Ammi, and I will be reunited.

We are allowed outdoors for half an hour before dinner. I inhale the air. I think of my bicycle at home, riding down our street with the red bougainvillea hedges on either side, a red scarf over my hair. It's almost dusk as I make my way to my palm tree. But there is someone in my spot today. A boy with steel-rimmed spectacles.

José.

Tears well up near the corners of my eyes and spill out. "How are you?" I ask.

He beams back at me. "I've been looking for you everywhere."

"Same," I say. I root in my pocket and find the friendship bracelet I made for him and have kept just in case. I hand it to him. "I made it for you."

He smiles shyly as he ties it around his wrist. "I won't take it off," he says as he twists a blade of grass through his fingers.

There is so much that I want to ask him. So much to say. We sit, our backs slightly turned away from the other children on the playground. "Have you been allowed to talk to your mother?"

"Once," he says. "There was a gas leak from a generator into Mamá's cell. She and baby María are in the infirmary now. But they're both okay and together at the Eloy Detention Center."

My stomach twists, but I'm relieved to hear that they're both safe. "My ammi still isn't showing up in the database," I say glumly. I smell the damp, freshly hosed grass and the spicy perfume of the flowers. I am frightened but I don't want to be doleful.

"Simi, Mama says that your mother was on the bus with her from Ajo to Eloy. She was sick, so they took her to a clinic in Ajo. But she's alive."

My hands are trembling with so many emotions. Relief, that she is alive. Fear, that she's been hospitalized. I can barely open my mouth to speak.

"I want to run away, José. I need to get out of here. We have a better chance of finding them on our own. I can't keep waiting for news."

"There's no other way," José says flatly. "We can do more research while we're in here. We just need to find the right moment. Don't run away," he tells me fiercely. I nod.

My heart is still racing with the news of Ammi. "Alright," I say, "but promise that we'll go together to look for our mamas when we get out."

"I cross my heart," he says with a smile.

We aren't allowed to touch each other so I can't hug him. Instead, we sit there as the sun sets, waiting for another day.

It is twenty-one days since my arrival at Casa Phoenix. The days are marked only by a sudden windstorm one day, a boy whistling on the street outside like the ice-cream man back home, my English teacher's wedding ring suddenly missing from his finger, and Paul growing a beard.

The only thing to look forward to is that Sophia has said she is going to talk to Paul. At my last session with her, she promised me that she was going to tell him to expedite my age verification and set up a call with my father.

"I'll tell him that it is necessary for your mental health. I will put it in writing," she told me.

That was on Tuesday.

On Wednesday, a judge ordered that Ana is to be reunited with her family. Because of the rules, we can't even hug. But as I say goodbye and wish her good luck, I notice that she still wears the bracelet I made for her around her wrist.

Now our shelter is more crowded, as more children pour in. There are well over four hundred children. Our room has bunk beds fitted in like pieces of a jigsaw puzzle. Eight of us squeeze into the room now. Each of us has a private space of four feet by four feet. I haven't seen José for days.

I sit in the common room reading my Gandhi book, anxious and worrying if José is even in the shelter anymore. How would I even know if he's left? It isn't until I happen to catch the date on one of the counselor's phones that I realize it's July 3. My birthday.

I am now officially thirteen.

No one will sing to me the way Ammi would have.

No one will bake a cake the way Nani would have. No one will dance with me the way Dadi would have.

I decide not to tell Sonia or Valería. I'm in no mood to celebrate.

Suddenly, I hear a voice call my name: "Simi Singh."

I get up and go the door, where a staff member is waiting for me. "Your age is verified," the man says with a broad smile. "The papers came in yesterday. You will speak to your sponsor today. I am taking you to the phones."

My sponsor.

Abbu.

CHAPTER TWENTY-TWO

It doesn't feel real. I beam, my smile spreading from cheek to cheek. Never would I have imagined this to be the greatest birthday present I would ever receive.

Thank you, great data gods.

Everything looks lovely as we walk to the phone area. I have to question whether I'm dreaming. The phone room is like a crying room for homesick kids who don't want to hang up. There are other children in line, breaking into tears upon hearing the voices of their parents.

Their voices all blend together while reality sets in.

Finally, it's my turn. I pick up the phone and punch in the numbers I've memorized by heart with trembling hands. My pulse races as I wait for Abbu to pick up. I pray it does not go to voicemail.

I hear a cough. A beloved clearing of the throat and the familiar long, drawn-out "Hellooo!" My father's loud, jovial voice sounds as if he is in the room with me.

I start crying, loudly, intensely. "It's Simi," I manage to say. But the sobs won't stop. We are only allowed to talk for ten minutes. Six hundred seconds. I have already wasted some of them. I pull myself together.

"Simi, beta . . . Are you okay??" Abbu chokes on a sob. I have never heard him cry before. "Rabb di Shukkar, Thanks be with God."

"I love you, Abbu. I don't want to be here." My voice quivers. A tear trickles down my throat. "I want to be with you and Ammi."

"Simi. Don't lose heart." His voice shakes. "I have found a lawyer. We are doing everything we possibly can. I love you."

"Me too, Abbu," I reply. Then I ask the one question on my mind, dreading the answer: "Abbu, have you heard from Ammi? Do you know where she is?"

I can hear his muffled cries, and my throat closes. I do not speak.

"No, Simi. We are looking every second of the day," he says.

I suck in a breath. I have to stay strong. That used to be Ammi's role in the family—to be cool, calm, and collected. I will think like her until she comes back. "Abbu, tell your lawyer to check on a Lucía Menezes in Eloy Detention Center. Picked up and brought to the Ajo station on May eighteenth or May nineteenth. She was with Ammi when we all got separated. She will know."

I can hear the excitement in his voice. "Yes, pucca. I certainly will." His voice is a little stronger.

Time is running out and I know I have to hang up soon. "I thought I would already have seen your face by now," I say as I choke on my voice. "How has this happened?"

"Be patient, Simi. You will be with me soon. My

lawyer has all the papers ready to show the authorities that I am your father. They will release you to me before month's end."

I sigh, that's only a week away and I have no faith in this slow and broken system to make that happen. But there is no other way.

Ten minutes is up in no time.

"Tell Nanaji that I have lots of books here," I say bravely.

"I will. I love you, beta. I can't wait to make a spicy aloo paratha for you when you come home. Is the food okay?"

"Not as good as yours," I joke. "Pranam to Nanaji, Nani, Dadu, and Dadi. Till next week, Abbu."

"Sat Shri Akal, Simi. Stay strong."

And then he is gone again.

I replay Abbu's voice in my head. *You will be with me soon.* But no sooner do my hopes rise than they fall yet again.

"Your father will need an affidavit from a court and from your grandparents in India," Paul tells me between sips of coffee that afternoon.

My eyes are fixed on Paul's wilted plant as he explains to me that on my birth certificate, my Abbu's name is spelled *Gurbir* while on his passport it is *Gurbeer.* If I am to be released, Abbu and I will have to prove we are related.

A month ago, I would have broken. But now I feel numb. What if these details take months? What else will they throw at us? I can hardly muster a reply. All I manage to say is "How long has it been since you've watered that plant?"

Paul turns around toward the snake plant in the corner. "I forgot about that one," he says.

I hand him my bottle of water and turn to leave.

I spend the remainder of the weekend trying to get an appointment with Sophia, but all the employees are on edge. Ten journalists are visiting Monday morning ahead of a congressional delegation in the afternoon.

News filters in. Children learn things from their parents on weekly calls and they tell other children. A senator had tried to come in two weeks ago and was turned away. This apparently led to a big outcry in the press.

Sonia and I, who have achieved big-sister status for good behavior, will be visible to the visitors. We are told not to speak to them.

My job is to stand near the cafeteria door and praise the food if asked.

But I plan to do something else entirely.

I stay up, writing a note in bed the night before the journalists arrive.

Dear Reader,

My name is Simi Singh and I am asking for your help. I am a thirteen-year-old from India and I've been here now for

32 days. I came into this country with my mother, Henna Singh, on May 14 through the deserts in Mexico, but she was separated from me in the desert.

We are escaping the Brotherhood party in India, who beat my father and smashed his knees for marrying my mother, who is from a different faith. My father, Gurbeer Singh, was finally given political asylum after coming to the US, but my mother and I were denied.

My mother is here. She may be in a place called Eloy. My father is here. He is a taxi driver in New York. I am in here in Arizona. Our family is split apart in three different places.

I miss my mother. I want to look for my

father. But I have only just been allowed to speak with him once after days and days, even though the rules say we can speak once a week.

My grandparents have always urged me to defend my beliefs. I believe that this system is wrong.

Do you agree? If you do, write your name and phone number and drop it near the cafeteria door, under the quote on the wall: "Observe good faith and justice toward all nations."

Below is my father's number.

Sincerely,
Simi Singh

I tuck the note inside my shirt pocket the next

morning. I've memorized the day's schedule. The reporters will be taken to see a tai chi class, then cross a basketball court, where some girls will be tossing a ball around, then go past the loading dock, to see children sitting in theater-style seats watching a Disney film. They are not to know that these are *for display only* activities accessible to us children when visitors come. They will pass a classroom. Boys and girls being taught English.

Then they will come to our cafeteria. A special meal of chicken and vegetables has been prepared for them and us. I am sure the chicken will not be rubbery, and the vegetables will not be soggy. After that, the journalists will be walked down a hallway where song lyrics and patriotic phrases are painted on the walls. *America the Beautiful. Liberty and Justice for All. I Have a Dream.* That's where Sonia and I are told to stand.

I look at the cafeteria clock. It's twelve thirty. They must be around the corner. I run my eyes over the room as the first batch of children comes and gets their food and the journalists trickle in behind them, holding pens and tiny blue notebooks, listening attentively as they walk in a huddle with our director and some senior shelter staff. They look at the children in line holding trays with Oreo cookies, applesauce, Jell-O, chicken, and mashed potatoes.

Their fingers point to some of the children while they ask our director questions. Our shelter lawyer tells them to smile so that us children don't feel like animals in a cage, and all I can do is shake my head.

I clutch the note in my pocket. My heart is beating a tattoo against my ribs as I study the journalists to determine who looks the most trustworthy. There is a young woman in bold blue glasses, who is dressed more casually than the others, in a white T-shirt and blue jeans. She has asked the most questions. She looks Indian.

As the group gets closer, my face begins to sweat and my heart thumps so loudly that I feel the whole cafeteria might hear it. They walk toward the door that opens into the hallway. I have strategically positioned myself near this exit. I smile at her, hoping she will notice. She does.

She says hello as she meets my gaze. I seize the

moment. I clutch the note in my sweaty palm and put my hand out to shake hers. "Hi," I say with a smile, as I slip the note into her palm. She is quick. There is a flicker of acknowledgment in her eyes as she wraps her fingers around the note. Her eyes seem to give me a nod before she walks on. It is the most meaningful conversation I've had with an adult in weeks.

Her footsteps grow softer as she walks away. I wonder if she will leave me her number somehow, if she will call my abbu. I wonder if her kindness is only her being polite.

Our director ushers the group toward the hallway, saying, "Now we will take you to the rooms where the children sleep."

"May I use the bathroom first?" a voice replies. It's hers.

The visitors wait in the cafeteria while an escort takes the woman across the hall to the toilet. I stand still, wishing I were allowed to hold Sonia's hand.

"Isn't the chicken good?" Sonia says to another reporter, who smiles in return.

Finally, the woman in the bold blue glasses rejoins the group.

"Shall we?" the director says.

There is a clatter. As the group walks off in a row, I notice that the woman has dropped her notepad a few feet in front of me. But she doesn't move to pick it up. It's only when I make the move to pick it up for her that she bends down as well. I feel a thin piece of paper slip into my hand. The thumping inside my ribs slows down. The heat recedes from my body. I stop sweating.

The woman nods and catches up with the group that winds their way through narrow hallways.

I wait until I am beneath my covers to read it. There are ten words.

I AGREE. I WILL DO EVERYTHING I CAN.
RINI BOSE.

Her phone number is written below her name.

My body sags with relief as I exhale at last.

CHAPTER TWENTY-THREE

I go unhurriedly about my routine the following day—class, afternoon chores, recreation. All I can think about is the piece of paper from Rini Bose that I keep in my pocket. I wonder what she's doing, if she is doing anything at all.

Tuesday, Wednesday, Thursday, and Friday pass. No news, no news, no news.

It's hard enough trusting myself to do the right thing. Now I'm finding that it's even harder to trust other people too. How can I know that Rini Bose will be true to her word? Or that there are people on the other side of Paul's computer looking for Ammi? Or even that thousands of miles away, Ashok is choosing not to bully the team? That Nanaji and Nani are safe from the Brotherhood?

I try to find ways to pass the time, to replace my negative thoughts with positive ones. Nani's sheekh kebab formula works only sometimes. I try to appreciate the small bit of nature around me. During the recreation hours, I watch a mockingbird hop around the yard as it seeks out insects. It stops every few feet to partly spread its wings, flashing its white patches. It repeats the same song, with varied and artful imitations, all day long. It reminds me of the days when I would meet Abbu and Dadu for lunch after they had plowed the field. We would eat saag, paratha, and pickles, watching the sparrows hopping around with twigs in their beaks that seemed to be twice the size of their tiny bodies. I remember saying that they would never be able to take flight with the weight of those twigs. They would soar off to build their nests. Dadu would explain to me that the bird is small but believes that she can fly. We're all capable of great things if we believe in ourselves.

At last, I get my weekly call with Abbu.

"Your journalist friend, Rini, called," he says. His voice is cheerful and full of hope.

My heart leaps.

"I'm so proud of you, Simi," Abbu says, pride in his voice. For the second time in a week, I hear my father cry. "You are such a smart girl. I've always said so. What did I tell you before I left? You are a captain wherever you go."

"Thank you, Abbu," I say, my heart filled with relief. "Did she find Ammi?"

"No—"

I flinch at the sound of the word.

"—but," Abbu continues, "she has submitted a request to the shelter authorities asking for a list of children who have been in the shelter for more than a month, even though their parents are in the US. Apparently that is illegal, to keep a family apart for so long."

"That's me alright."

"My lawyer says these shelter people are scared of bad press. They will move our file quickly now."

"So far, I haven't seen anything move quickly," I remind Abbu.

"But now we have Rini too. Did you know she is also Punjabi? She plans to dig into your case specifically when she has the list."

"I'm glad we found her," I say.

"*You* found her," Abbu says, his voice full of pride, and I have to stop myself from grinning ear to ear. Our time is nearly over.

"I wish there were a way to speak to Dadu, Dadi, Nani, and Nanaji," I say.

"They all got together to call me after I finally heard from you. They miss you so much, Simi. They're praying for Ammi's return every day."

I tour our living room at home in my mind; I see the

chintz curtains, the patchwork quilts, the flowery upholstered sofas with blue piping, Dadi's gramophone, Nani's kebabs, and the cream-yellow French doors opening onto the lawn. I can even open drawers in the kitchen and see the forks and knives neatly arranged the way Ammi had laid them. I can see my grandparents sitting around the kitchen table having a cup of tea as they talk with Abbu.

One day we will be back together. In the meantime, I have to hold my head high.

"Love you, Abbu. I will see you soon."

This time I believe it might come true.

By Monday morning, it seems as though the system has finally activated. Everything happens so fast. I am told by Paul that I'm going to be collected by a social worker to be escorted to my father in New York on Friday. All my paperwork is processed.

My heart sings a song. The letter to Rini actually worked!

I skip out of his office, bubbles of excitement floating through my body.

I can see myself sitting up in bed with a big tray across my lap filled with breakfast from Abbu. I can see a yellow earthenware dish on the tray with a bowl of homemade yogurt next to it. A hot paratha stuffed with potatoes, spicy mango pickle, and Abbu's signatures: eggplant mashed in mustard oil and garnished with green chili on the side. If I close my eyes tight enough, I see both Ammi and Abbu sitting at the edge of my bed asking me about my day.

When I open my eyes, I see kids my age waiting in line to talk to someone—anyone who can tell them where their parents are. What will happen to everyone else?

But as I walk back to my room, I can feel that something is different in the air. The staff seems a little less bossy. The children a little more boisterous. The shelter is overall more bright.

The journalists' visit must have triggered something.

I soon learn that Sonia, Valería, and Anita are all told that they too are leaving in the next few weeks. During recreation hours we sit in a huddle and talk about the clothes we will wear, how we will style our hair, the food we will eat when we are out in the real world. Sonia and I promise that we will stay in touch. I give her Abbu's number and address.

The only person I haven't been able to find is José.

The sun is heavy in the sky on the evening before I am scheduled to leave. At recreation time, I walk to my palm tree. The days are long here and light shines through the leaves.

"Well," says a familiar voice. José stands in front of me, eyebrows cocked, his hands in his pockets, a bit like the first time I met him.

We grin at each other without saying a word. Relief floods my heart and veins. I couldn't imagine not being able to say goodbye. We've only just met, yet it feels like we've been by each other's side for a lifetime. I brace myself to tell him that I am leaving. But that I will get

Abbu and Rini Bose to get him and his mother reunited as fast as possible too.

"I have news!" we both say at the same time.

"You go first," I tell El Leader.

"My sponsor is coming to collect me tomorrow. It's my uncle. My father is undocumented, so he can't sponsor me. But they have agreed to let my uncle take me to my father. He is a farmer near here."

I jump to my feet. I want to hug him, but because I'm not allowed, I let out a whoop, a laugh, and a cry instead. "I'm flying to New York to be with my abbu. Also tomorrow!"

José claps his hands together.

We both become quiet. It's like we're both feeling the same thing: How is it possible to be so happy and so anxious at the same time? Even if it means finally reuniting with Abbu, my heart breaks at the idea of flying thousands of miles away from where Ammi is. She feels so close yet so far away.

"I haven't heard a peep from my mother since she went to the infirmary," José says, as if reading my thoughts. "Or news about my baby sister. I haven't been allowed to call my father. I don't even know if he knows that Mamá is inside Eloy."

I reach my hand in my pocket to fish out the sheet of paper from Rini Bose and hand it to him. "When you get out, call this number," I say. I tell him all about Rini Bose, the note I gave her, the calls she made. "Tell her where your mom is and ask her for help." It makes me feel better to know that José will be here. We are still a team, even with an entire country between us.

José looks at me and smiles. "I should call *you* El Leader," he says.

The sky turns pink and orange as the sun continues to fall.

After a moment, I realize that we are really going separate ways this time.

I do my best to smile. "Phone when you reach home. You have Abbu's phone number. Okay? We have to find our mothers together."

José nods. "I promise. One last fact: Nine million people live in New York."

"Adiós, amigo. Till we meet again."

We stand for a moment looking at each other. I see my friendship bracelet on José's wrist, his honest green eyes, his hair now long and curly around his neck. I close my eyes to imprint it in my mind, storing it away until I see him again.

One day I will take José to India and my peepal tree. Ammi will be there too. She and Lucía will have a picnic of their own. So will Dadi and Dadu, Nani and Nanaji, Ravi and Reena. I will even invite Ashok. I think about the food that I would pack for us as I fall asleep that night, dreaming of the yellow mustard fields.

I wake at six the next morning without the sound of banging. I have already packed my things, but I unzip my backpack to take out my Gandhi book. I open the page and touch my leaf for luck.

My roomies give me all kinds of notes and messages for their family outside since I'm the first to leave.

Valería breaks rules and hugs me. Then everyone decides to break the rules as well. Sonia and Anita promise to meet me in New York one day.

A staff member breaks up our goodbye and tells me to wash and dress quickly. I don't have much time. Drawing a comb limply through my tangled hair, I look around the room with all its pasted notices and rules one last time.

Valería has jumped into bed again. She does not want to say goodbye. "Who will tell me stories?" she says, her voice muffled.

Sonia and I smile at each other. "I will," Sonia says.

I know that they will always look after each other.

Sophia is the one to meet me in the hall and escort me to Paul's office. She produces a piece of cake and a fork. Her eyes look at me with kindness, unlike how they look at Paul when he isn't moving fast enough. "I'm proud of you," she says with a smile.

We walk together through the halls for the last time. I imagine what it will be like to take a long shower, wear loose cotton clothes, sit at the kitchen table with my father. Suddenly, I wonder what America will really be like outside of what I've already seen. Is it just as strict and regimented out there as it's been in here?

"What is it like on the outside?" I ask Sophia.

Sophia takes a moment to answer. "I think you'll find that there are good people everywhere," she says.

I give her a nod, my mouth now full of cake.

CHAPTER TWENTY-FOUR

I'm in the sky for the second time in my life, looking down at the skyscrapers of New York poking through the low hanging clouds. The social worker escorting me home on the flight takes me to a taxi when we land, and there is a part of me that expects the driver to be Abbu. The pickup area at our terminal is just as crowded as the airport drop-off area was in Delhi when I last saw him disappear into the crowd.

"I am taking you to a shelter," my escort says. I nearly

scream. "Just for the night. Tomorrow you will be medically examined, introduced to your legal team, and by evening your dad will pick you up," she details.

I am so on edge, waiting to see Abbu again at last, that I almost forget to look out the window. We cross ill-laid pavement and dirty roads, pass shabby brown brick buildings, some with boarded windows, and then turn onto a wide avenue, with vendors on street corners, tall buildings with shining shop windows, and an endless throng of hurrying people.

We get off in front of one of the many tall buildings and take an elevator to a floor so high I feel I'm back on the plane. There is a fresh set of clothes on the bed. It's all very different from Casa Phoenix.

The sun floods into my room the next morning, its rays dancing on my bed.

Today is the day I will finally see Abbu.

The morning and afternoon stretch on and on. I watch the agonizingly slow clocks tick away as I'm shepherded from office to office to examination room, answering the same questions again and again, waiting for Abbu's scheduled pickup at five o'clock.

The waiting is unbearable.

At 3:30, they are done with their questions at last. I wait on a hard chair in the lobby, facing the doors, counting the minutes. The sunlight is strong, almost fierce.

I smell his familiar scent of coffee and aftershave even before the glass doors push open.

Abbu wears a festive pink turban and his same wide smile as he walks into the waiting room, tears threatening his eyes, and I know then that I love him more than life itself. I quickly rise to my feet, the book I have been unable to focus on falling to the floor.

"Abbu!" I scream.

His arms are wide open. I run into him and inhale his scent.

"You're taller! I'm going to have to feed you well," Abbu declares. He has such a look of love in his eyes that suddenly everything feels worth it. We cling to each other. There are others in the room, but I don't care. For the social worker, it must be a common scene.

"I prayed to all the gods every day," Abbu says. "And now we will pray together."

I know that he is talking about praying for Ammi. I'm so happy, but at the same time I feel the same empty hole of Ammi not being here with us. I don't want to annoy the gods, wishing for more when I have Abbu back at last. "I'm here. I'm not going anywhere," I say, even as I too wish Ammi was here with us right now.

Abbu puts his hands on my shoulders and steps back to look at me properly, tears pooling in his eyes. "My lawyer is already in touch with a person in Tucson, where the Eloy Detention Center is," Abbu says. "They still can't find Ammi in their system. But we will not stop looking."

I try to stay strong, but when I look at Abbu I can tell that he looks older, even after only a few months. His face has formed new lines and wrinkles. There are lines for me and lines for Ammi. They are lines of worry, fear, determination. Suddenly, I remember the puppy that Ammi and I found in the road on the way to school so many months ago. I remember the look on its mother's face when she thought we might take her puppy away from her—hair standing on end, teeth bared, her eyes determined not to let go. *Abbu and I can't live a day without you,* Ammi had said. Abbu's new wrinkles remind me of the dog's face. And I know that Ammi is somewhere right now, her eyes pleading for me.

Abbu's yellow cab sparkles in the bustling street, full of street vendors, crowds of people, and brightly lit storefronts. "I hosed and vacuumed every corner to welcome you," says Abbu proudly.

"Ammi will love it," I say, strapping on my seat belt.

We drive through streets lined with skyscrapers, then gold-lit brick buildings. Schoolchildren cross the street; people are dressed in smart clothes. We drive through a tunnel. The rows of cars ahead of us give the illusion of a silver, swaying waterway. Then we drive down a humming street with Indian shops and restaurants.

"There is a little India here. You can get all our spices

and vegetables. Anything you want," Abbu says, catching me staring. We have not stopped talking for a second.

"When Ammi comes, it will be very easy for her," I say, manifesting her return.

We both have a million questions, a thousand plans, hundreds of ideas. I chatter so fast that one sentence gets caught with the next.

"Slow down. I am in no hurry," says Abbu. "I want to know every minute of everything." He reaches out to clasp my hand in one of his as he holds the steering wheel with the other.

We wind our way out of traffic and through streets lined with trees and one-story houses.

"Welcome home," he says, stepping out and opening my door.

I follow Abbu up a few steps, through the door, and into a hallway. We take off our shoes Indian-style and walk into a bright living room. On the table under the window are photographs of Ammi, me, Dadu, Dadi, Nanaji, and Nani in beautiful silver frames. There is one of Ammi and me on a tractor on the farm. Of

Dadu and Dadi sitting stiffly on the couch in our living room. Of Nanaji sitting in his library, Nani and me standing at his side.

Another table on the side is set for dinner with floral mats and blue flowers in a jar. Just the way Ammi set the table at home.

My stomach growls.

"Let me get you dinner," Abbu says. Abbu has wisely kept the food plated and ready to be heated. In thirty seconds, I have a meal of hot parathas and butter chicken in front of me. I fold the paratha around a chunk of the chicken, breaking it with my fingers.

Abbu plays my favorite song, "Eena Meena Deeka," on his phone. For a moment I imagine that Dadi will be there next to the gramophone dancing while Dadu lets out a jovial laugh.

My heart swells with memories of Nanaji savoring each bite while Nani warns him not to eat too much.

Suddenly, my appetite is gone. I'm about to push my plate away when a choir of voices seems to sing my name.

"Simiiiiiiii!"

I swivel my head around to see the faces of my grandparents starring back at me through Abbu's computer. Their eyes are moist and glistening. Abbu's hands shake as he places them down on the kitchen table.

Dadi, Dadu, Nani, and Nanaji are huddled around their own kitchen table, fighting back tears. Their voices race each other for volume, thanking the gods for my safety. I take in the images of each of them: Nani's rosy cheeks, Nanaji's twinkling black eyes, Dadu's yellow turban, Dadi's sparkling salwar kameez that is as bright as her smile.

Miraculously, I am hungry again.

There is so much to ask them. Nanaji has gotten a new pair of spectacles. Nani has started baking classes in a women's NGO, and Dadu and Dadi are engrossed in a new TV show about a girl my age who becomes a pilot. The wheat has been planted at the farm. It will be ripe by Diwali. I speak with a full mouth as the familiar tastes of butter, garlic, turmeric, and chicken melt on my tongue. Finally, I push the plate away from me.

"I was so scared. I thought I would never see you all again," I confess.

Nanaji leans forward. His eyes are serious. "We would have searched every inch of the desert until we found you," he says for all of them.

"Just as we will not stop searching for Ammi?" I respond, jutting my chin out in determination.

"Of course we will never give up," Abbu says firmly. "She is the sun, and you are the moon."

Before I forget, I pull out the Gandhi book from my things. Nanaji and Nani share a look of pride. I lay it on the table and flip through the pages until I find my peepal leaf.

"Such a flimsy leaf," I say. "Somehow it made it all the way across the seasons, the oceans, the border, the desert, and all the way to New York. She will too."

Thousands of miles away, the elders nod.

I can spy our terra-cotta Ganesh statue peeking out as it seems to wink at me. Our two kitchens become one.

CHAPTER TWENTY-FIVE

Abbu and I make call, after call, after call. In India, Dadi, Dadu, Nani, and Nanaji do the same. Never did I think that I would speak to so many government workers, so many lawyers. We make call, after call, after call.

"Is there a Henna Singh in your system?"

"Have you seen anyone who meets this description?"

"Please call us back if you have any information."

Finally, at last, the phone rings.

Abbu is at his usual morning spot near the cooking

range, a steaming cup of coffee on the counter next to him, as he lunges for it.

I tune out everything as I wait with bated breath, praying hard inside myself. *Please, let it be news of Ammi.* I study the steam from Abbu's coffee as I wait. Through the open window, our street smells like cheese and sounds like a stormy ocean. Car engines, horns, sirens, and screeching tires resound permanently in our two-family structure.

"It's for you," Abbu says. He passes me the phone and I put it to my ear.

"Simi," begins José uncertainly, as if he's not sure if I am there. "Hello?"

I can hardly believe it. I nearly forget to say hello back. "Yes, yes! It's me, José. How are you?" My breath catches in my throat. I feel I will break down if I speak more.

"Simi, she's here," José says. His voice is a high-pitched squeak. I put the phone on speaker. Abbu seems to sense my excitement and stoops down to hear. "You mother is here in Eloy, where my mother and baby sister are as well."

Something shatters. Abbu's coffee mug has slipped from his fingers. Both of us ignore the coffee and glass everywhere. A cool wave washes over me, like the soft drizzle of spring, easing the tension in my limbs. I taste the salt of tears as I let go.

"Is she in good health?" Abbu shouts louder than he probably means to.

"Are you *absolutely* sure?!" I screech.

We both speak simultaneously.

"I'm absolutely sure," José says. He tells us everything he knows. Ammi had been taken into Eloy with Lucía and baby María.

"But is she okay? Why she is not in the system?" asks Abbu, his gentle voice a bit shaky.

"She is okay. Mamá tells me that she has lost her voice, and her documents were taken from her before she crossed the border," José replies. "No one knew who she was."

I will the blood to return to my veins and focus on the most important piece of the news. Ammi is alive and we know where she is.

"My mother was exposed to a gas leak that sent her

to the infirmary. Your mother was there too. She's been there the whole time. My mother has tried to confirm her identity," José continues. "My mother told everyone that the lady who has lost her voice is Henna Singh. But they won't listen to her."

Abbu seems to have stopped breathing.

I fire off question after question. "What comes next? What should we do? How can we get them out?" There is a long silence at the other end.

I look over at Abbu. He cradles me in his arms for a few seconds. I listen to his heartbeat as I gather my thoughts.

Finally, Abbu speaks. "Ammi is alive and in good health. Your mother is alive and in good health, José. We can thank all the gods for that," Abbu says. "Now, let's get to work."

CHAPTER TWENTY-SIX

"I've submitted a request for a visit to Eloy," Rini Bose says through the phone.

She is the first phone call we make, and the first to get back to us. She tells us that she's doing everything she can to make the approvals go faster so that she can try to see Ammi and Lucía and talk to someone face-to-face about how to get them released.

From India, Dadi gives a thousand thanks to all the gurus. Dadu is convinced that bad days are behind us.

Nani and Nanaji squeal with relief and then flood us with questions that we don't know the answers to.

"I've listed José's mother among the people I want to visit. I'm not allowed to add Henna to the list since she's not in the system," Rini says when she calls us back. "But is there any way I'd be able to recognize her?"

I shift on my perch on the kitchen stool.

Abbu and I both speak at the same time. "We have photos."

I suddenly remember one more thing as Abbu texts her the photos. "My name, Simi, is tattooed on a heart on her left wrist."

Abbu blinks back tears. "I had forgotten."

"That's extremely helpful, Simi," Rini says. "I will be in touch as soon as I know more."

It's Abbu's lawyer who calls back first to schedule a video call. When we join the meeting, both his and Rini's faces beam back at us.

"You have very strong-willed friends," our lawyer says. "Rini has managed to beat the bureaucracy and pay a visit to Eloy today. She took photos of a tattoo on Henna's wrist and marched them right up to the right people."

"Thank you, Rini!" I cry.

"Don't just thank me," Rini says. "There was a nurse at the infirmary who was already making a stink by the time I arrived. It seems you've made quite a few friends over the past few months."

Abbu looks at me quizzically. And then it dawns on me. I remember the nurse at Ajo Detention Center who reminded me of Dadi as she checked me for lice. I had given her Ammi's name. She'd told me that she would do her best to look for her. It all feels like another lifetime.

"She works for the Coast Guard and was volunteering at the infirmary where Henna has been kept," Rini continues. "She'd already tracked her down when I arrived. Both of us have agreed to speak as witnesses on Henna's behalf."

I am awestruck and confused at the same time. "Witnesses for what?" I ask.

Abbu's lawyer clears his throat. "Well, there is good news and bad news. The good news is that Henna is finally in the database," he says. "The bad news is that she has now been moved from the infirmary to Eloy Detention Center and will be tried for illegal immigration."

I can't take it anymore. My ammi, Henna Singh, has already been through so much. She applied for political asylum. She should not be in prison like a criminal. It isn't right.

I am tired of optimism. I want my mother back.

"What can we do?" Abbu begs.

The lawyer shuffles through options and words I barely understand. They talk about applying for something called a trafficking visa. They weigh one option against another, but every option sounds like it will take forever with no guarantee.

I squeeze my eyes shut and clench my fists under the table, determined not to cry.

"Is there any other way?" Abbu asks finally.

"Yes," the lawyer replies. "She can be released against a bond of ten thousand dollars."

You could hear a pin drop.

"It's an impossible sum," Abbu whispers. "How will I ever come up with that kind of money? I am down to my last penny. We are already so deep in debt."

I close my eyes so that I don't have to see his devasted face.

Simi, don't lose heart. I will be back with you shortly. Ammi's voice echoes in my head. Soon I can no longer hear it, just a ringing in my ears. I open my eyes and see Rini looking at me with a worried brow.

"Are you okay?" she asks.

I don't know if I could speak even if I tried. Nevertheless, Rini somehow hears my heart call out to her.

"Well," Rini says, taking a deep breath, "let's do it. Let's raise the money through crowdsourcing."

My mouth falls open. "How?"

"We will tell people your story. They will be

saddened, angry," Rini says. "Let's give them a chance to do something good."

"How do I tell people my story?" I ask.

Rini smiles back at me. "If you're willing, you can start by writing it down."

CHAPTER TWENTY-SEVEN

I sit up in my bed with a notepad in front of me, writing in lamplight.

Everything in my bedroom is almost exactly like my room in India. Posters of my favorite musicians are on the wall, the bookcase is painted the same color, the curtain has a flowered pattern, and the desk has photos of Ammi, Nanaji, Nani, Dadu, Dadi, and all of us together.

I write as much as I can before I forget it all. I write for

Ammi, but I also write for José, Sonia, Valería, Anita, Ana. I write for everyone I've met since I left home.

I'm the daughter of a Sikh dad and a Muslim mom, born in India. My parents love each other so much, but some people there think their love is wrong. Those people beat up my dad and threatened my ammi. I didn't want to leave. Who would? Nobody wants to leave their family, their home, or the land they belong to. But home wasn't home anymore. It wasn't safe.

We came to America so we could be together safely as a family. My abbu came first, but when my ammi and I applied for asylum to join him, they said no. So my ammi and I had to cross the desert between Mexico and Arizona to be with him. That's where my ammi was lost to me.

I've missed my grandparents, my friends, my school, my hockey, the food, the language—everything. But the hardest part was not knowing if my ammi was even alive.

Now I know she's alive, but she's out of reach again because of an indifferent SYSTEM that's keeping her in prison! They want a $10,000 bond. We don't have that kind of money.

I try to recall as much as I can. I write down what it felt like to walk thirty miles through the desert; I write about the cages at the detention center, the aluminum blankets, going days without a shower, the list of rules on the shelter walls, and the way Paul would recite his script about the system. It makes me feel better to know that somewhere, Sophia is putting him in his place. I think about Pablo, the guard who I played a game of Scrabble with, and the nurse who never stopped looking for Ammi. When I finish wringing out all the memories, I email what I've written to Rini with my blessing.

Outside my window, a cat streaks across the alleyway. It looks so much like one of the strays that prances across our garden back home. I wonder where its ancestors are from. Nature does not create fences or walls between countries like we humans do.

Finally, I tuck myself into bed and stare up at the night from my window.

Ammi always used to tell me to look for the brightest evening star. No matter where we live, anywhere in the world, it is always there. Venus. It's our star.

I ask the stars to shine more brightly on us.

CHAPTER TWENTY-EIGHT

"So Abbu and I have to raise all this money to get Ammi," I relay to Ravi and Reena over FaceTime the next day. How I have missed our chats.

"Did you not see?" Ravi asks, his large glasses magnifying his eyes. It's evening in India and morning in the US. Ravi and Reena are hours ahead of me.

Reena sends me a link to a Facebook post.

A photo of Ammi and me holding hands appears on a donation campaign with a goal of $10,000. *Bring This*

Family Back Together: Help Reunite a Mother with Her Daughter. Beneath the goal, I recognize my own words.

Simi's story: I am the daughter of a Sikh father and Muslim mother . . .

My eyes scan the page. There are already over one hundred donations with accompanying messages. There are notes from friends in India, names I recognize and names of people who thank Ammi for nursing their wounds and their children's wounds. A group called Mothers United has posted the campaign on Facebook. Donations roll in from all over the US from people I've never met: in Arizona, Atlanta, California, Georgia, North and South Carolina, Virginia, Tennessee, Texas, New York. A familiar but unexpected name catches my eye.

Ashok donated fifty dollars.

In the comments section he has written:

Stay safe. We are on your team.

I can hardly believe it.

By noon, we have reached our goal with over four hundred donations.

I beg Rini to keep the drive going so that we can raise the same amount for Lucía and María's return to José and his father. She tells me that she has already set up a separate fund just for them that's well on its way.

José and I talk on the phone. His mother and baby sister have finally been released and sent home. We both squeal with glee and conjure up plans to visit each other one day.

"I want to see New York," he says.

"I want to show you New York," I reply.

"Rini," I say that night while Abbu and I FaceTime her. I heave a huge sigh. Another worry has dawned on me. "Without her documents, no airline will fly her. And we can't afford to go there. It will take forever for her paperwork to be processed."

Rini smiles her warm smile. "There are other ways."

A pool of volunteers and online donors have offered to help Ammi journey across the US. Abbu and I huddle over a map and chalk out a route for Ammi's road trip from Eloy to Queens with designated stops. We select drivers and hosts.

I remember what Sophia, my counselor at the shelter, said before I left. *I think you'll find that there are good people everywhere.*

The drivers are a female priest, the granddaughter of a Holocaust survivor, a schoolteacher, a housewife, a waitress, and a nanny. The hosts are outraged mothers in Arizona, New Mexico, Oklahoma, Missouri, Illinois, Indiana, Ohio, and Pennsylvania. Some will keep a hot lunch ready, others a warm bed.

By dinnertime, the complicated operation is set up. For the first time since I stepped into America, I see its famous speed, efficiency, and humanity.

At 8:30 a.m. in Arizona, 11:30 a.m. in New York, and 9 p.m. in India, two moms from Mothers United wait at the gate of Eloy Detention Center to pick Ammi up. Ravi and Reena sit with Nanaji, Nani, Dadu, and Dadi, making sure our group FaceTime is flawless.

We watch through our screens, as one of the mothers records the moment for us, streaming it live for all of us to witness. We hold our breath as Ammi steps out of the prison, her eyes scanning the crowd. The other mother walks up and gently hands her a phone.

Ammi's hands shake as she takes the phone.

She tries to speak, but nothing comes out.

"Hello, Ammi!" I cry.

"Hello, my Henna," Abbu says at the same time.

Tears stream down Ammi's face. She holds the phone close to her face, blowing kisses into the receiver, her silent sobs saying everything she can't. Her voice is gone, but her love comes through loud and clear.

As the call ends, we know the hardest part is over, but her journey home is just beginning once again. Ammi's silence weighs heavy on us, but so does the hope of her coming home. The plan is in motion, and now we focus on the road ahead—every mile bringing her closer, every stranger along the way becoming a part of her story.

We take shifts to monitor progress, alert the drivers if there are traffic snarls, and keep hosts updated of the ETA. It seems that all of the US has opened her arms to Ammi. It's more than just a road trip; it's an act of love and solidarity. People we've never met are offering their cars, their homes, and their time to help reunite our family.

She spends nights in the homes of strangers; someone feeds her, someone clothes her, some just chat with her. Everyone does what they can to help her rest, heal, and reach us.

CHAPTER TWENTY-NINE

Abbu and I share pizza and ice cream after the sun goes down, settling into the moment we've been waiting for. We sit together on our front stoop as I begin to dream aloud of what we will do when Ammi finally gets home.

"I want to show her the golden fountain near Central Park," I say.

"I want to take her to the beach. I want her to see the ocean and feel free," says Abbu.

I picture her walking on the beach, her long hair flying in the wind, a trail of footprints behind her . . . She is holding my hand on the right and Abbu's on the left. She is safe between the two of us. I feel a peace that I have not felt in ages.

A car comes to a halt in front of us. Its windows are tinted, but I can already feel that it is her.

For a second, I freeze, watching Ammi step out. Ammi's gray eyes gleam with happiness and relief. Her black hair is tied in a braid, longer than it's ever been. Her salwar kameez hangs a bit on her.

The street is unusually quiet, as if the world is holding its breath along with me. Abbu is standing, a tender smile across his face. I'm not sure if this is real or just another dream where I see Ammi, only for her to vanish again.

But then Ammi's arms wrap around me, and I feel the warmth of her skin, the steady beat of her heart. Her familiar scent—like jasmine and home—fills the air. That's when I know. She's real. The softness of her breath on my hair, the slight tremble in her grip—it's all too real to be a dream. Tears spill down my cheeks, and I hold her tighter, afraid to let go. She's really here.

Everything is blurry.

Ammi is thinner, but her hug is just as strong as it's always been. And then, like a miracle, I hear it—her voice. For a second, I'm not sure if I've imagined it.

"It's beautiful, Gurbeer," Ammi says as she looks up at our new home. "But it could use some flowers."

"We can plant them now that you're here," Abbu replies.

That night, after hours spent talking and holding one another, Ammi and Abbu adopt their familiar tones and tell me to wash up for bed. Even though the little girl of three months ago is gone forever, I happily do as I'm told, blissfully content to be a child once again.

A LETTER FROM THE AUTHOR

Dear Reader,

Thank you for picking up *The Freedom Seeker*! This book is very special to me, and I hope that as you read it, you'll connect with Simi's story and the challenges she faces. At its heart, this is a story about courage, love, and the power of hope—even when life feels insurmountable.

At the beginning of Simi's journey while still in India, Simi's family faces religious intolerance—where people decide that they don't like that her parents come from different faiths. As a result, their family is targeted by a group that tries to hurt them just because they believe in something different. Sadly, there are many families in the world who are forced to flee their homes for similar reasons, whether it's because of their religion, ethnicity, or political views.

When Simi and her mom decide to leave India and travel to the US, their journey isn't easy. Crossing the desert is dangerous. They have to trust people called coyotes, or human smugglers, who promise to guide them safely across the border. But many times, these smugglers lie or take advantage of people. Simi and her mother face harsh conditions like extreme heat and exhaustion, making their journey even more difficult. After they cross the border into the US, things don't get easier. Simi and her mother are caught by border patrol and separated, and Simi finds herself in a detention center without any ability to contact her father or other family members.

This part of Simi's journey is similar to what many real-life children go through when their families try to cross into the US in search of safety. You might have heard about things like this on the news—about families being separated at the border or about children waiting in detention centers for months. It's important to understand that these aren't just stories; this is something happening to real people, just like Simi, right now.

But even though Simi faces these challenges, *The*

Freedom Seeker is also about how, even in hard times, there are people who care. In the story, there are employees and volunteers who help Simi and other kids. There are people who work hard to reunite families and give them hope. Simi's mom gets help from strangers who shelter her and guide her safely back to her daughter. Their kindness shows that even when things seem unfair, there's always room for love and good people willing to help.

When I wrote *The Freedom Seeker*, I thought a lot about the families who come to the US looking for safety. Some of them are escaping dangerous situations in their home countries, just like Simi. They leave behind everything they know, hoping for a better future. But sometimes, when they arrive, they face new challenges and have to figure out how to make a new life in a place that can feel cold and unwelcoming. Simi's story is about holding on to hope, even when life feels unfair, and finding the courage to keep going.

I wanted to share this story with readers like you because I believe young people are powerful. You have the ability to understand and care about others, no matter how different your experiences might be. Maybe you've seen stories about immigrants on the news or heard about families separated at the border. I hope this book helps you understand what it feels like to be in their shoes. It's important to remember that even the smallest acts of kindness can make a big difference in someone's life.

Simi's story is about finding home—not just in a place, but also in the people we love. It's about standing up to bullies, believing in yourself, and understanding that love and kindness are more powerful than hate. Through all of her challenges, Simi never gives up hope. She learns that there's always strength in community and in the people who care about us.

For those of you who have experienced immigration yourselves, I hope this story helps you feel proud of your journey and the bravery it takes. And for those of you who haven't, I hope *The Freedom Seeker* helps you see how important it is to be kind, to stand up for what's right, and to understand that everyone deserves to feel safe and accepted.

Thank you for joining Simi on her journey. I hope her story inspires you to think about how you can be a force for good in your own community—whether by helping a friend, standing up to a bully, or learning more about people who may have different experiences than you. Even small acts of kindness can make a big difference.

Ruchira Gupta

ACKNOWLEDGMENTS

Stories take shape through the voices we carry and the people who lift us along the way. *The Freedom Seeker* is the result of many who supported, challenged, and believed in it.

Along the Mexico–Arizona border, I met brave individuals whose names I cannot mention for their safety. The NGOs and humanitarian workers fighting for migrants and asylum seekers are the true heroes of this book. Their work is unseen by many, but lifesaving for countless others.

Migration is not just the theme of this book—it is my family's history. My husband, Sunil Narula, is Punjabi, with a Sikh father and Hindu mother. His family was uprooted during Partition and protected by their Muslim neighbors in what is now Pakistan until they could safely leave for India. The quiet strength and deep connection to history of his parents have shaped my own understanding of resilience.

In Queens, Sikh gurdwaras became sanctuaries for lost and frightened immigrants navigating an unfamiliar city. Their spirit of compassion is at the heart of this story. With their support and that of the New York State Council on the Arts, I conducted theater workshops with immigrant communities, learning firsthand what home means to those seeking refuge.

This book was shaped by the generosity of many. Sarina Shah, a brilliant high school student I met through Books of Wonder, strengthened it with her sharp feedback. Nandana Sen, a fierce advocate for women's and refugee rights, has been a steady force in my life, and her work with the Women's Refugee Commission continues to inspire me. Rattanamol Singh Johar and Kalpana Raina provided invaluable insights into life in Chandigarh.

I am deeply honored by the support of Alan Gratz, Leymah Gbowee, Jason De León, Aida Salazar, and Abigail Disney, whose endorsements mean the world to me. I first encountered Jason's research through Saloni Mathur and Aamir Mufti, whose introduction led me to his groundbreaking work on forced migration.

None of this would have been possible without my editor, Sam Palazzi, whose sharp eye and patient guidance helped shape this book. Nor without David Levithan, my publisher, who believed in this story and gave it a home. My agents, Samantha Haywood and Laura Cameron, guided me in ways big and small, ensuring this book reached the world.

I am forever grateful to my parents, Vidyasagar Gupta and Rajni Gupta, whose belief in me has never wavered. Their love keeps me going, reminding me that stories must serve justice.

And always, to Gloria Steinem, the friend who has walked beside me on this journey of storytelling and activism. Her unshakable commitment to truth and justice continues to inspire me every day.

To everyone who helped along the way—thank you. *The Freedom Seeker* belongs to you.

ADDITIONAL RESOURCES

Resources for Readers of *The Freedom Seeker*

Thank you for reading *The Freedom Seeker*! Simi's journey takes her across borders, both physical and emotional, as she navigates challenges related to religious intolerance, immigration, human smugglers, family separation, and a foreign country. The issues she faces are experienced by many people around the world today, and this resource page is here to help you learn more about these important topics—and find out what you can do to make a difference.

Understanding Religious Intolerance and Celebrating Diversity

In *The Freedom Seeker*, Simi's family faces challenges because her parents come from different religious backgrounds. They are targeted by people who don't accept their love because of religious intolerance. Religious intolerance happens when people don't respect others who have different beliefs, and it can lead to bullying, harassment, or even violence.

What Can You Do?

- **Ask questions:** Don't be afraid to ask questions about different religions or beliefs. Understanding helps create respect.
- **Celebrate diversity:** Learn about the different cultures and religions in your community. Try learning about the holidays your classmates or neighbors celebrate.
- **Stand up for others:** If you see someone being bullied because of their religion or background, speak up or tell a trusted adult. We can all help create a more inclusive environment by standing against intolerance.

Discussion Questions:

- How does Simi's family handle the bullying they face because of their different religions?

- Why do you think it's important to respect other people's beliefs?

Books & Movies to Explore:

- *Does My Head Look Big in This?* by Randa Abdel-Fattah: A relatable story about a Muslim girl navigating identity and religious tolerance in high school while deciding to wear the hijab for the first time.
- *The Faithful Spy* by John Hendrix: A graphic novel about Dietrich Bonhoeffer, a German pastor who stood up to religious intolerance during World War II.
- *Ten Things I Hate About Me* by Randa Abdel-Fattah: This book explores themes of interfaith relationships and identity struggles in a young girl hiding parts of her culture and religion from her classmates.

Learning About Immigration and Refugees

When Simi and her mother leave India for the US, they face the challenges of immigration. People leave their homes and cross borders for many reasons—some are escaping violence or persecution, while others are searching for better opportunities. Simi and her mother, like many immigrants, must cross dangerous terrain (the desert) and place their trust in smugglers, who don't always tell the truth or keep them safe. Immigration can be very difficult, but it is also filled with hope for a better future.

What Is a Refugee?

A refugee is someone who leaves their home country because it is no longer safe for them to stay. They may flee because of war, natural disasters, or persecution for their race, religion, or beliefs. Like Simi and her mother, many refugees seek asylum in other countries, hoping to find safety and stability.

Challenges Migrants Face:

- **Crossing borders:** Migrants often face dangerous conditions when trying to cross borders. Some, like Simi, have to cross deserts or rely on human smugglers, who can be untrustworthy.
- **Separation from family:** Families are sometimes separated when they arrive in a new country, as Simi and

her mother were. It can take a long time to reunite.

- **Detention centers:** Many migrants are placed in detention centers while they wait to be processed. Conditions can be cold and harsh, as Simi experienced.

What Can You Do?

- **Learn about immigrant stories:** Ask family or friends if they know of anyone who has immigrated, or explore books and movies about migration.
- **Support refugee organizations:** You can help by supporting groups that work to assist immigrants and refugees.

Organizations That Help:

- **UNICEF:** Works to help children worldwide, including refugees.
- **International Rescue Committee (IRC):** Provides support to refugees fleeing crisis.
- **Kids in Need of Defense (KIND):** Offers legal help to unaccompanied migrant children in the US.

- **Women's Refugee Commission:** Seeks to improve the lives and protect the rights of women, children, and youths displaced by conflict or crisis.

How You Can Make a Difference

The Freedom Seeker is about standing up for what's right and finding the strength to keep going, even when times are tough. You can make a difference in your own community, just like Simi learns to do in the book.

Acts of Kindness:

- **Welcome newcomers:** If you know someone new to your school or neighborhood, make them feel welcome by saying hello or inviting them to join your group.
- **Learn about new cultures:** Take the time to learn about the cultures of people around you. Ask questions, show interest, and celebrate differences.
- **Stand up for others:** Whether it's bullying at school or seeing someone treated unfairly, standing up for others is one of the most important ways to show kindness.

What Projects Can You Do?

- **Hold a donation drive:** Work with your school or community to collect donations for refugee families in need.
- **Create a "welcome to our community" kit:** Help new families by creating kits with helpful information and resources about your town, like maps, important phone numbers, and local attractions.
- **Write letters of support:** Work with your class to write letters to organizations that help refugees or immigrants, showing your support.

Get Inspired:

- **Watch:** PBS Kids has great videos about kids who have immigrated to new countries and their experiences.
- **Read:** Explore books like *Front Desk* by Kelly Yang or *Esperanza Rising* by Pam Muñoz Ryan, both of which feature young immigrant protagonists.

GLOSSARY OF KEY TERMS

asylum officer: An immigration officer who interviews asylum seekers to determine if they are eligible for asylum in the United States

asylum seeker: A person seeking protection in another country because of danger in their home country

border patrol: A law enforcement agency responsible for patrolling the borders of the United States

chain immigration: When an immigrant to the United States sponsors other family members for admission—such as parents, children, and siblings

coyotes: Smugglers who help people cross borders, often illegally and unsafely

detention center: A facility where immigrants are held while they wait to be processed or released

immigration: The process of moving from one country to live in another

migrant: A person who moves from one place to another, especially in order to find work or better living conditions

refugee: A person who has left their home country to seek safety or protection

religious intolerance: When people are not respected or are mistreated because of their religion or beliefs

smuggler: Someone who takes goods or people into or out of a country illegally

unaccompanied minor: A child (or person under the age of eighteen) without the presence of a legal guardian

vigilante: A person who takes the law into their own hands, without legal authority